THE SACRED LITERATURE SERIES

POEMS OF HANSHAN

The Sacred Literature Series of the International Sacred Literature Trust

Poems of Hanshan

TRANSLATED BY

PETER HOBSON

WITH AN INTRODUCTION BY

T. H. BARRETT

Professor of East Asian History, School of Oriental and
African Studies, University of London

Published in cooperation with the
International Sacred Literature Trust

ALTAMIRA
P R E S S

A Division of
ROWMAN & LITTLEFIELD PUBLISHERS, INC.
Walnut Creek • *Lanham* • *New York* • *Oxford*

For more information about the
International Sacred Literature Trust,
please write to the ISLT at:
1st and 2nd Floors, 341 Lower Addiscombe Road
Croydon CR0 6RG, United Kingdom

Photoset in Sabon by Northern Phototypesetting Co. Ltd, Bolton, UK

ALTAMIRA PRESS
A Division of Rowman & Littlefield Publishers, Inc.
1630 North Main Street, #367
Walnut Creek, CA 94596
www.altamirapress.com

Rowman & Littlefield Publishers, Inc.
A Member of the Rowman & Littlefield Publishing Group
4720 Boston Way
Lanham, MD 20706

PO Box 317
Oxford
OX2 9RU, UK

British Library Cataloguing in Publication Information Available

Library of Congress Cataloging-in-Publication Data

Hanshan, fl. 627-649.
  [Poems. English. Selections]
  Poems of Hanshan / translated by Peter Hobson ;
  with an introduction by T. H. Barrett.
    p. cm. — (The sacred literature series)
  Includes bibliographical references.
  ISBN 0-7591-0414-X (alk. paper) —
  ISBN 0-7591-0415-8 (pbk. : alk. paper)
  1. Han-shan, fl. 627–649—Translations into English.
    I. Hobson, Peter, 1924– II. Title. III. Series.

PL2677.H3 A26 2002
895.1'13—dc21   2002015068

Printed in the United States of America

⊖™ The paper used in this publication meets the minimum requirements of
    American National Standard for Information Sciences—
Permanence of Paper for Printed Library Materials, ANSI/NISO Z39.48–1992.

INTERNATIONAL
SACRED
LITERATURE
TRUST

The International Sacred Literature Trust was established to promote understanding and open discussion between and within faiths and to give voice in today's world to the wisdom that speaks across time and traditions.

What resources do the sacred traditions of the world possess to respond to the great global threats of poverty, war, ecological disaster, and spiritual despair?

Our starting-point is the sacred texts with their vision of a higher truth and their deep insights into the nature of humanity and the universe we inhabit. The translation program is planned so that each faith community articulates its own teachings with the intention of enhancing its self-understanding as well as the understanding of those of other faiths and those of no faith.

The Trust particularly encourages faiths to make available texts which are needed in translation for their own communities and also texts which are little known outside the tradition but which have the power to inspire, console, enlighten, and transform. These sources from the past become resources for the present and future when we make inspired use of them to guide us in shaping the contemporary world.

Our religious traditions are diverse but, as with the natural environment, we are discovering the global interdependence of human hearts and minds. The Trust invites all to participate in the modern experience of interfaith encounter and exchange which marks a new phase in the quest to discover our full humanity.

Contents

Professor Barrett and the International Sacred Literature Trust are grateful to the family and Executors of the late Peter Hobson for their help and permission to publish Peter Hobson's translation of the *Poems of Hanshan*.

Introduction

"... read the real writers, read Balzac, Han Shan, Shakespeare, Dostoevsky."
(Jack Kerouac to Philip Whalen, 16 January 1956)*

Hanshan, "Cold Mountain," was the pseudonym adopted by an unknown hermit poet in China over 2,200 years ago. The poems collected under his name have had an immense impact in East Asia, especially among Zen Buddhists, and have been translated many times into Western languages.

We know that Peter Hobson would not have objected to the publication of his own translations of some of these poems, since in 1977 he included three of them in a small magazine which he helped to run with some friends, but his main aim in translation seems to have been to capture the spirit of the originals in English simply for his own personal satisfaction. Yet his striving for what he termed "sincerity," preserving the intent of a poem rather than making a fetish of literal accuracy, has bequeathed versions whose freshness and immediacy surely deserve a wider audience.

So rather than risk detracting from his achievements by adding explanatory material, I have made only minimal changes to his text, despite its occasional references to Buddhist and other terms, such as samsara—most easily defined as the opposite of nirvana—and to Chinese names in Japanese form. Thus "Kanzan" is the Japanese rendering of Hanshan, and "sennin" (often translated as "an immortal") is a Japanese word for a practitioner of the macrobiotic arts. "Cold Mountain" has been particularly popular in Japan, and we can prove that Peter Hobson worked from the best Japanese anthology of these poems.

*In *Jack Kerouac: Selected Letters, 1940–1956*, ed. Ann Charters (Harmondsworth: Penguin Books, 1996), p.542.

Despite the deftness of touch that is present throughout these transla-tions, the reader may notice an occasional insipid or clumsy phrase that seems at first sight to undermine the poems' overall strength. These appar-ent infelicities cannot be attributed directly to their author or authors, for examination of the Chinese originals behind the "absolute" cur of poem 4, line 6, or the "lovely" sound of poem 19, line 5, for example, reveals that the epithets have been brought to the poems by the translator out of thin air. Similarly, the "incessant" road of poem 10, line 2, is actually no more than "endless" or "limitless", while the curious "headcloths" of poem 21, line 4, turns out to stand for an embroidery flower used as a hair ornament. From what we know of Peter Hobson's cultural and pro-fessional background it seems unlikely that the examples quoted are lapses due to carelessness or ignorance. My own guess is that the theory of translation which he espoused freed him from close linguistic imitation of the Chinese, but still obliged him to transmit the flavour of the corpus of poems as a whole. Perhaps we might read these occasional quirky turns of phrase as a reminder that the Hanshan corpus was transmitted for its content rather than in accordance with Chinese notions of formal perfection as poetry.

The original order of Peter Hobson's typescript has also been preserved: it corresponds to that of no other Chinese source or translation, but appears to embody a certain amount of thematic grouping of poems which no doubt reflects his considered intentions. For those who would like to know more than the translations themselves reveal, I have provided a sketch to show the place of these poems within the history of East Asian religious verse ("Hanshan's place in history", p.115), and also a guide to other versions ("Hanshan in translation," p.147). The numerals in paren-theses at the head of each poem translated, which represent the running numbers of the poems in a well-known Chinese reprint, may be used as a key, as explained in the latter section, in order to consult other versions. The asterisks against some of these numbers mark out a "late" rhyme scheme, a problem explained in the historical sketch.

I term the essay that follows the poems a "sketch" quite deliberately: other translators, assuming an existing interest in East Asian matters on the part of their readers, have been content to comment more on the immediate context of these poems, so that as far as I am aware no survey of the broader tradition to which they belong has ever been attempted. Literature is not my field, and the exigencies of preparing these transla-tions for publication have not allowed much leisure to improve my knowledge. Conscious of the tentative status of many of my remarks, I have therefore annotated this section the more carefully, so that serious students with a knowledge of East Asian languages will be aware of the reasons for my statements, and hence able to detect any misjudgements.

It may be that Peter Hobson would not have agreed with my own remarks on Hanshan, which are made from the viewpoint of one interested in the history of religion; perhaps he would have found them simply uncongenial. Even so, they are offered here out of the deepest respect for his own talent, and in the conviction that it has been a privilege to help in bringing his work to a wider readership.

THB

Poems of Hanshan

1

(15)

From father and mother
                ancestral plenty
of fields and orchards;
              no envy of others;
the click and clatter
            of my wife's loom
and the babble of children's
                first inchoate speech;
hands beating out time
              to the dance of flowers
and my chin
          cupped to the song of birds;
and no guests
           applaud our happiness except
the woodcutter
           on his occasional rounds.

2

(27)

A rustic
      living
           in a beam-and-thatch dwelling
has few
      horses
         or carriages at his gates,
but in deep
      woodlands
          the wild birds gather
and the broad
      valley streams
          are full of fish;
he takes
      his children
         to gather bramble-berries
and his wife
      to help him
         husband his fields;
back
      in his home
         he has nothing to treasure
except
      the books
         piled high on his bed.

3

(111)

When young,
                I took the scriptures
                                to the hoeing;
in those days
                elder brother
                                shared our house;
but when
                the countryfolk
                                thought fit to disapprove
and even
                my wife
                                began to look askance at me,
I left
        their transient
                        world behind
to wander
                where a man
                                may read his books in peace.
Like a fish
                stranded
                                in a wagon-rut—
could no one
                have spared a little water
                                and let me live?

4

(222)

In my home village
everyone found me incomparable,
but I have been in the city
only one day and already
find myself compared
to an absolute cur –
because my cloak
does not billow enough
or because my shirt
is a little too long!
They've no respect;
I'm keeping my falcon hooded –
let sparrows go on the rampage!

5

(184)

"What a yokel!
what a scarecrow!
what a
silly
little hat!
and how tight
his jacket is! . . ."
What's
really tight
is cash—not
so much out of
fashion as
out of
basic
means; just
watch me when I'm rich!
I'll wear
a whole
pagoda on my head!

6

(99)

Wretched
          poor scholars
hitting
          the limits in
cold and
          hunger,
existing
          unattached for
love of
          writing verse,
grinding
          their bones to
pound out
          words . . .
who's
          interested? The
writings
          of a derelict
have no
          takers. My friend,
pen your
          sublimities
on fancy cakes
                    and put them out
for hungry
          dogs to eat—
even they
          won't touch them.

7

(148)

A personable fellow,
master of the six
traditional arts,
yet hounded from the south
up to the north
and driven from the west
out to the east,
versatile as a wisp
of floating weed
and mobile as a
puffball in the breeze,
distinguished by both
lineage and breed—
first name "Stony"
second "Broke."

8

(173)

Alas!
now poor, now ill,
destined
to cut all ties
with family and friends, no
cooked rice
in the pot, the
kettle
full of dust, thatched
hovel not
impermeable to rain, a
lumpy bed
hardly
conducive to a good night's sleep
—no wonder
things have come to this; too
many sorrows
dissipate a man.

9

(250) *

What is it makes for
constant melancholy, if not
the knowledge that our lives
are like a fungus growth
decaying in a day?
How can we tolerate this
endless game from new to old,
to withering, to dying?
To think of it is
to be trapped within regret,
which is a deadly sentiment
that nothing can dispel
save all casting off
bodily experience,
repairing to the mountains
and there hiding oneself.

10

(28)

To ascend this cold mountain path
is to climb an incessant road
along the endless valley, boulder-strewn,
and across the wide river
fringed with heavy reeds;
the moss, without the moisture
of the rain, is treacherous
and pines, without the urging
of the wind, sing out:
"Whoever dares to put the world aside!
come sit with us,
amid white cloud!"

11

(300)

Some thirty years this side of
                    being born, a
thousand times ten thousand leagues
                    of questing,
traversing every river through
                    the blue grass plains,
riding the red dust-clouds
                    on the barbarian fringe,
yearning for immortality
                    through the occult and alchemy,
seeking for clues
                    in the Classics and dynastic history,
until today. Now
                    the return begins on this
Cold Mountain.
                    I shall lay my head
beside its streams
                    and wash the dross of time away.

12

(130)

Birds singing
       with intolerable sweetness
have surprised my sleep;
         now
from this arbour
       I can see
the incandescent
       crimson of the cherry tree,
the sleek
      plumage of the willow,
sunrise cradled
       in the blue divide of hills
and clouds immaculate
       in the emerald lake;
who would have dreamed
       that simply
by leaving the world behind
       I could ascend
and reach the sunny side
      of old Cold Mountain?

13

(293)*

Life is so easy here
beneath Cold Crag, whose
indrawn mysteries
amaze me still;
basket to hand I leave
to gather herbs and come back
with a pannier berry-filled,
and laying out the rush mat
sweet and soft, I nibble
like a bird at tender shoots;
washing a gourd out in the
limpid lake, I simmer
herbs into a thick ragout;
then sit back in the sun
drawing my robe about
to browse awhile
among the ancient poets.

14

(282)*

Amid a thousand clouds and
ten thousand waters, one
gentleman of leisure
by white day roaming
green hills, by night sleeping
back at the foot of the crag,
thus passes springs and autumns
in solitude, gathering no stain;
what joy! – to depend on no one,
quiet as the depths
of a river in autumn.

15

(285)

High, high on the mountain-top
where horizons are boundless, I
sit alone and unknown; the orphan
moon is caught in the icy pool
– but no, the pool is empty
and the moon is in the sky;
therefore I improvise this song
– simple, with no Zen in it.

16

(210)

Like still waters silent
as crystal, translucent
to their very depths, not a single
thing stirs in my mind
and the worlds stop turning;
no sully rising in the heart
time's aeons are negated
and immutable; knowing
how this can be, I know
the Truth without shadow.

17

(100)*

Endeavouring to find a simile
for life and death
I think of ice and water –
water hardening into ice,
ice melting back to water; if
all death becomes inevitably life,
life turns to death again;
one cannot wound the other –
each makes the other beautiful.

18

(55)

These peach-blossoms look fair
to outlast summer, but storm
and the moon hasten them on
and will not wait; we look
in vain for the men of Han
– all are gone; and gone
are the flowers that fade
and fall, and gone are mortal
men who pass and change;
where today this dust dances
an ocean flowed in former days.

19

(228)*

See how the peak of Tendai
is tall and solitary, raised
above all others; the wind
sways pines and bamboos with
a lovely sound and the moon appears,
defining the sea's tide; I gaze
down to the blue mountain's edge
where the white clouds talk to me
of subtle things; I was right
to leave the world of crowds
for the mountains and waters,
but how my heart longs
for a friend along the way.

20

(281)

Sitting today before the high crag,
in time the smoke-mist settles
till the clear valley is one
cool path where jewelled mountains
thrust upwards a thousandfold;
the morning shadows are still
and clouds are white; in night's
brightness floats the shining moon;
my person is unsullied by dust
or stain; what is it makes my heart
so sad?

21

(169)*

Once
 briefly leaving
   my mountain hermitage
I went
 into the royal township,
    saw
the usual bevy
  of elegant
    femininity –
fair faces
 lovely figures
   headcloths like clouds,
cosmetics
  touchingly applied,
     eyebrows like swallows' wings,
gold bangles,
  cunning ornaments
    of silver flowers,
fine
 silken dresses in imperial
    reds, purples, pinks,
features
  as glowingly unreal
    as fairy goddesses
and the moving air
   a sea
    of heady perfumes,
making
 all men wonder,
   watching with heavy eyes
dyed
 in the colours
   of mad infatuation
finding
 in this glittering show
   something

incomparable
                and irresistible
                                that binds them heart and soul
and forces them
                to follow after;
                                dogs
do the same –
                a rotten bone
                                will have them slavering
and licking
                teeth and lips;
                                in lack of circumspection,
men and dogs
                are much alike;
                                see
this white-haired crone
                caught in the treadmill
                                of senility,
tottering
        like a ghost;
                a canine mentality
will never
        carry us beyond
                our temporality
into the realms
        of pure
                release.

22

(35)

The third month,
silkworms are still small
and girls go flower-gathering;
leaning on walls
they sport with butterflies
or look in pools
to pelt the drowsy frogs;
plum-blossom heaped
in sleeves of light brocade
and bamboo seedlings
culled with golden combs
– how lovely!
and how trivial it is!
I like it better
than my Cold Mountain.

23

(245)*

My whole life
                has been nonchalant
and easy, hating
                  the heavy-handed, loving
the light touch so that
                    whereas
other men
            have mastered mighty
mercantile matters
                  I
own
      one volume of the scriptures
not even
            properly bound for
ease of carrying
                as I come and go; for
medicine presupposes
                  some sort of illness
but I
      taking samsara as it comes
keep my heart unblemished
                  and see
light, lightness
        and the Divine
Wisdom
        everywhere.

24

*(119)**

A cottage in the rice fields

       to escape

          the heat of high summer,

and a pitcher of wine

      but no

        fellow wine-bibber;

therefore in desultory fashion

       I take

          a heap of nuts, seat them

before me, pass them

      the wine and

         – on my lonely reed mat –

play the host,

     our main dish being

         a bowl of plantain leaves.

Soon, they're all

     quite tipsy!

        I cup my chin and stare

at a heap of children's marbles

        lying there;

each one

   is

    Mount Meru.

25

(106)*

Of loveliness
               of lakes and mountains
there are fold
               upon fold of emerald
landscapes, all
               refracted in the haze
of evening and
               the air is soft, and damp
upon this flimsy
               headcloth;
a glistening
               of dew lies on the straw
I've wrapped
               around my shoulders;
I am shod
               in seven-league sandals
and I grip
               a staff of aged wisteria,
but here I stop
               and gaze beyond this world's
dead dust
               into the realms of dreams;
if only
         I could reach them!
But what
               difference would it make?

26

(101)

I remember
      the days of my youth –
how I delighted
        in the open
hunt across the high plateau
          and
never thought of asking
           for the post
of District Mandarin
        much less
of pondering things spiritual
         but
leaping
     mettlesome to the chase
rode my white horse
        and coursed the hare
and loosed my sky-blue falcon;
         who
would have dreamed
        that hoary age would come
soliciting the compassion
       of younger men?

27

(175)

Noble intentions
once laid down
cannot be folded!
and I am not a mat
for you to squat upon!
I wander headlong
through the wooded hills
and rest alone on
the recumbent rocks.
You come to me
sweet-tongued
and urge me to accept
some public office; then
with gifts of gold and jade
beg me
to pull my fences down
and sow a crop of weeds!
It really is quite pointless
– please, begone!

28

(102)

I rest and sleep
                in the deep forest
but am by birth
                a farmer's son
brought up to see
                the simpleness of things,
not twisting my speech
                to flatter a man;
I do not look
                to jewels for my surety
but you have yet
                to find the pearl you seek.
You are a plenitude
                of flowing waters;
open your eyes
                and see
the wildfowl
                dancing on your waves!

29

(232)*

I have observed
                    how men of mediocre minds
amass great wealth
                    in real estate and grain,
drink wines
                    and slaughter living flesh for food
and say: "I am
                    content to be so prosperous."
Not knowing
                    that the pit of hell is deep
but trusting
                    in high Heaven's clemency
they heap themselves
                    a Himalayan peak
of evil karma; how
                    will they avoid
the stinking flames
                    of nemesis?
A businessman
                    drops dead – his family
go wild
          with bogus grief; priestly
professionals
                    intone the sutras over him
and goblins
                    and ghosties
are vastly
                    entertained, but no
Elysian fields
                    are opened up to the deceased
by this performance
                    of bald-pated monks.
Ah! how much better
                    had he seen the light
before he faced
                    black hell! For as

no raging winds
        can shake a sturdy tree,
true hearts need not
          anticipate catastrophe,
nor any favours either.
              I address
these words
        to headless fools. Take heed!
and read
        what I have written
time
     and time again!

30

(290)

Only white clouds for Kanzan,
Solitary, not specked by dust,
a straw mat,
a mountain hut,
a single lamp,
the moon's wheel,
a stone bench
facing blue lakes, and
tigers and deer for friends;
he tells himself he rejoices
in quiet obscurity,
but would love to be, at length,
quite outside phenomena.

31

(11)

Spurring my horse past a great

                     mansion long deserted

my traveller's mind is moved

                     to memory of its denizens;

high palisades, low

             fences in ruins,

great gravestones, little

               tombs broken down,

wind-torn cactus

           shaking its own shadow,

the yew trees sighing endlessly

                    – ah! how undistinguished

were the men whose bones

                sleep here – not one

who merits mention

           in the records of the saints.

32

(247)*

Yesterday I visited
          Cloud-haze Ashram,
saw the sennin adepts
              in crowns of stars
and draped moon-cloaks
            insisting
they lived close to nature.
              I asked them
about their arts –
          "Quite beyond words!
mystical, magical!
           unsurpassed!
Our elixirs
        are most esoteric!
We do not die
        until the white crane comes!
We ride
      on the back of a leviathan!"
I found these statements
          hardly edifying
– in fact
      without rhyme or reason;
shoot arrows into space,
           they fall to earth.
These sennin adepts
          are like ghosts guarding a corpse.
The moon of the heart
        has an essential light
quite beyond any
        mere phenomena.
Why seek
      the sennin's art?
The primal deity
        is in your Self.
To consort
      with fancy sennin
is to wed foolishness;
         do not get involved!

33

(284)*

One
    drift of the times
        that honestly
deserves a laugh –
      kids
        who leave home to rough it
nobly assuming
      that by opting out
          they're on the Path
togged out in gear
      that indicates
        detachment
from the world's
    vulgar dust
      though not
from its fleas;
    one feels
      that a homecoming
to the inward heart
      would surely be
        far more princely.

34

(229)

Four or five
                addled adolescents
pretentious
                therefore irresponsible
– not yet read
                ten books between them –
have the nerve
                to challenge age and
call the works
                of notable Confucians mere
sets of rules
                for brigands! Such are
our modern
                worms and weevils;
they reduce
                substantial volumes
to pulp.

35

(212)

To talk of food
          will leave you hungry
to talk of clothes
           will leave you cold;
eat the food
       and be full,
wear the clothes
         and be warm.
Deep pondering will not do
or saying that the Buddha
is hard to find; turn
inward to the mind –
the Buddha is there;
do not stare
outward.

36

(33)

One is told
that worries are hard to dispel
– one is told;
others hold
more optimistic views, yet
yesterday's worries
that I thought forgotten
are here again today
to plague me!
The moon wanes; worries
do not wane; the year
is renewed and
worries are renewed;
beneath a spring bonnet
walks a heavy heart
with last year's worries
lying leaden upon it!

37

(276) *

This cold crag is high
and steep, and so much
the better for that, for
no men come this way;
the high white cloud
covers my cave in silence
save when a monkey howls
across the green mountain
summits; let me stay
solitary, to grow
old in solitude!
Cold and heat bring
changing appearances,
but let the pearl of the heart
remain inviolate!

38

(59)

I strain my eyes
look far and wide;
the cloud is white
but endless. While
these crows and owls
are glutted and gleeful,
phoenixes and peacocks
starve and are pitiful;
pure-bred stallions stumble
on little stones while
plodding camels reach the palace gate – why so?
I cannot ask high Heaven
the reason why; perhaps
the lakeside chaffinch knows.

39

(298)

Tell me, my friend, how long
can leaf-borne flowers last?
Today's sweet blossoms fear
the hands that gather them;
tomorrow all will fade
and each be swept aside.
How sad is lovely youth
that the years turn to age!
Our world is like these flowers
– its bloom does not endure.

40

(230) *

Boisterous as the mountain-tops,
a fine fellow deferring to no one,
glib-tongued with the Vedas,
exegetist of the scriptures
(Confucian, Buddhist *and* Taoist),
mind closed to pangs or doubts,
iconoclast, damning all rules,
claiming the licence of a superman,
calling himself a "paragon",
of whom fools sigh in admiration
while wise men stroke their palms and smile.
Pie in the sky!
Cloud-cuckoo land!
How will such an oaf
escape death's desolation?
Not made for it!
Not an inkling! – forget him,
sit still and strive
to cut the bonds of anguish!

41

(110)

To hear him talk
                you would think him a superman
with skills and accomplishments
                      far outstripping
Confucius and Duke Chou;
              but look at that
dull visage, that unimposing form!
                  – a presence that not even
rope, halter and spurs
              could stimulate to action,
exactly like
          Duke Yang's pet dancing crane
embarrassingly immobile
              when his guests came
– great beak
        honk-honking at the crowd.

42

(129)

A well-bred boy
            – good-looking too –
compendiously well read
                in history and Classics
whom friends call
            "the professor"
for his universal
            scholarly repute
can neither win
            a civil-service post
nor turn a tender hand
                to farming;
winter finds him
            in a threadbare gown
wondering why books
                have let him down.

43

(80)

Slavishly

  he sought to expound

    the three Dynastic Histories

and slogged his life out

   on the five

    Confucian Classics

till age

  caught up with him

    and now he is

a petty civil servant

   still

    in bond

to yellow county office files

   and dead

    White Papers;

why

  could he not

   have turned his industry

to horoscopes

   and been forewarned

    of what

a constellation

   of inauspicious starts

    were his?

Even the

  weeping willow

   coming to life

just once a year

   does

    better.

44

(113)

Calligraphy: passable
Powers of judgement: reasonably mature;
in other words
impeccable qualifications for office
except that the examining board
took an almost personal dislike to him
and started digging for flaws.
Of course
Heaven's verdict must be invoked;
he should sit again this year;
a blind bowman may
with Heaven's blessing
hit the sparrow's eye
so – who knows? – he may well
scrape a pass this time.

45

(207)

Death is not kept at bay
                          by studying books
nor even by poverty;
                          what is the point
of literacy except
                          to get ahead?
A fellow cannot hope
                          to have an easy
life without it; it's
                          a flavouring
he spreads on life's
                          unpalatable
actualities to
                          numb the mind – a kind of
all-purpose
                          garlic sauce.

46

(208)

The slanderer
           slurps water
into a wicker
           basket;
one basket
           full
flees home
           in a spurt,
finds it
      gone –
that's how
           I see him;
the slandered
           victim
slumps back
           like an
onion plant
           in a garden plot
that men
        kick and pick
daily;
      next year
by the grace
           of Heaven
he is still
           surviving –
that's how
           I see him.

47

(104)

A rich man's party
>> at the high
>>>> hall
and the glitter
>> of a thousand
>>>> flower-lanterns
induce one
> candle-bereft
>> stranger
to crash the party;
>> his shadow
>>> betraying him,
they drive him out
>> to crouch
>>> once more in darkness
the fools
> reckoned
>> that with one more
eye to feed
> they would never have
>>> enough
light
> to go
>> round.

48

(94)

Wise men are never covetous;
fools love to rape the earth
for metal ores;
                    if
agricultural real-estate
obsesses some, this bamboo garden
is my very own;
                    why
sprain your back in search of
silver, break your teeth on
teams of horses, hordes of slaves?
Remember
            that, beyond the city-
limits, pine and yew mark out
vast lands reserved for graves.

49

(280)*

The long line of philosophers!
none could out-talk mortality;
born but to die, all suffered
inevitable dusty change;
their bones are piled as high as
Mount Vipula, lapped by vast seas
of weeping, pain and parting,
proving that no philosophy
can break the wheel of birth and death.

50

(98)*

Men maintain
            that in the investigation
of problems
            the truth can be invariably
ascertained –
            however intractable matters
may appear –
            by deftly applying opposing
arguments,
            meaning, I fear,
that their "pros"
                        produce good out of bad
while their "cons"
                        negate everything positive.
In this way
            all conceivable nonsense may
be sustained
            by the sophistic interplay
of half truths,
            one out-balancing the other.
For my part
            I prefer the immediate
feel of things,
            and no theology will ever
prove for me
            that hot is cold.

51

(220)*

My contemporaries all
agree I must be mad
though mine is not
a face to draw men's glances
and my clothing
is the standard hermit garb;
but what I say
they do not understand
and what they say
is not worth my reporting;
all travellers
who feel the need
are free to come
and see me on Cold Mountain.

52

(161)*

My dwelling has a single
inner room, nothing therein
save pure, resplendent emptiness,
the majesty of many suns;
sparse food to nourish frail mortality,
rough robe to cloak illusive corporality;
You thousand sages!
show yourselves to me!
Here is the Buddha of Celestial Truth
– mine!

53

(289)*

I see men's fingers turning
the pages of the Classics, perusing
other men's speech for understanding,
turning their tongues without turning
their hearts, so that tongues and hearts
are all turned back to back;
but if the heart is true
with no twists or turns,
tangles are untied
and knots undone;
look, therefore, to your Self,
seek none
to act on your behalf!
Self-mastery
brings knowledge with no ins or outs.

54

(178)*

I declare to travellers upon the Way
that your journeying out
is empty agony of soul;
men have in them a thing
of essential mystery,
unlettered and unwritten,
which answers shrillingly
when called, though hidden
inexistent in a secret place.
I tell you again:
Cherish the thing!
Guard it from wound and stain!

55

(165)

Carefree I visit
          the mountain monk;
ten thousand upon ten thousand
                    smoke-wrapped hills;
the Master himself
            points out the path home;
the moon hangs –
          one wheel of light.

56

(31)

"dark dark"	Kanzan's path
"plip plop"	cold mountain stream
"jug jug"	birds everywhere
"hush hush"	no men about
"sear sear"	the wind on my face
"thick thick"	snows cover me
"morn by morn"	I see no sun
"year by year"	I know no spring.

57

(39)

White crane pecks
              at bitter peach
resting on a journey
                 of a thousand leagues
to the mountains
              of the Blessed Isles
wanting
      fresh provender;
not yet arrived
             wing feathers fall
losing him
        his flight companions;
desolate returning
            to the home nest
his wife
      no longer knows him.

58

(66)

Tight-lipped not uttering a word
you sit; how will you speak
                        to men who come after?
Living in retirement in a clump of
forest, how will the sun of your
                        knowledge shine?
Be sparse and thin,
                not hard and brittle!
Harsh winds and frost
                will finish you,
who plough a stony field
                with a wooden ox
– no good grain
                ever grew from that.

59

(179)

Last year when birds sang in spring
I thought of my brothers;
this year when chrysanthemums
make autumn lovely, I think of new
life. Blue waters moan
in a thousand places, and yellow
clouds spread flatly all about.
How sad! my whole life's span,
remembering my life in the capital,
I shall break my heart.

60

(177)

When I think back
           on all the
things I have seen
            and done and
the fabled places I have
               visited –
for love of mountains scaling
                    ten thousand peaks
for joy of water sailing
               a thousand boats
escorting lovers to Lute
               Valley, and
mandolin in hand making for
                  Macaw Island –
who would have dreamed
             that now I
should live alone beneath
              the sighing pines
hugging my knees against
              the winter cold?

61

(154)

To this cold mountain
with its many mysteries
men are afraid to climb.
The moon shines on dark
waters till they gleam;
the wind-blown grasses
have a hunted air;
the withered plum trees'
flowers are snowflakes;
tree-stumps wear
the swelling clouds like
leaves – one burst of rain
then every scene is bright;
without the lightness of
fair weather, none can climb.

62

(176)

This remote retreat of mine
has mystery and a depth
of solitude hardly explicable;
tendrils are quivering
although there is no wind,
and long before the evening falls
the bamboos are in twilight;
and for whom do these slow
waters moan and the hilltop clouds
stand suddenly so still?
And midday finds me
still at rest inside my hut,
till suddenly
I feel the sun come out.

63

(168) *

This cold mountain comprehends
a self-contained dwelling;
compartment-less, six doorways
open out to right and left;
the blue empyrean is seen
within its hallway – each
chamber empty as the air,
the eastern wall flush
with the western wall,
and therein not a thing
(lest anyone come a-borrowing!).
And when the cold arrives,
I kindle grass for heat;
if hunger seizes me,
I boil up herbs to eat.
I do not imitate
this country aristocracy
with barn and byres and mansions
full of attachments leading them to hell
(that path once entered,
all is lost).
Think long and hard,
think hard and long!
The rules of my order
are not hard to grasp.

64

(30)

White cloud
             sails high above
the mountain-tops
                      and the green-reflecting
waters shudder
                  with tiny shocks
as there comes
                  the intermittent sound
of a fisherman
                  pounding on his oar
and singing
              snatches of a song
that my ears
              can hardly catch
– small sound
                  which tears my heart apart
like the
          sparrow's song
which sometimes
                  pierces like an awl
through the very
              roof of my house.

65

(18)

The old year
        goes
casting its sorrows
            on the coming year
but spring
        brings fresh colour to things;
the mountain flowers
          laugh at the verdant waters;
bees and butterflies
         are happiness itself
and birds and fishes
         are utterly lovable;
friends came to see me –
         the joy of them
so
   lingered that
from evening to dawn
         I could not sleep.

66

(235)

A man's life
        lived in dust and haze
reminds me
        of an insect in a bowl
that squirms
        around all day but never
leaves
    that bowl's circumference.
To be
    a sage or an immortal
is quite
    beyond me; anguish
beyond
    all reckoning is mine;
my years
    and days have fled
like flowing water; suddenly
I find
    that I am old.

67

The only man to know
habitual content
is one who leaves the world
for woods where flowers
grow like tall brocade
and every season brings
the freshness of new shades
of colour; looking
towards the crags he sees
the sweet circle of
the cassia trees, and thus
knows happiness, save
that the world and people
come ever to mind.

by Shide

68

(48)

All day
and day by day
it's like I'm drunk –
the rolling years
all flow away;
so let me lie
beneath the cemetery weeds;
what a dull, dark dawn I'll see!
My flesh and bones
will crumble, soul
and vital spirit
just about evaporate;
and when my mouth
is biting the iron dust
I'll be too sick
to recite the Classic
of old Lao-tze.

69

(223)

That the terms of life and death
are fixed by fate,
and that wealth and high estate
are Heaven's gifts – such
are the teachings of the ancients;
but I will not perpetuate
enormities of this sort!
A man of clear perception
prays for life to be short;
the idiot longs
for life to be prolonged;
a lunatic is fat
with wealth and fruitfulness;
the man of sense is penniless.

70

(64)

How broad and great
are the waters of
this Yellow River
drifting eastward
endlessly onward in a
sublime and clouded flow, while
men's lives, no matter how
prolonged, come to a
stop!
In truth
they would love to mount
the high white clouds
but how shall they grow wings
when even in the time
of black-haired youth
to move and to be still
at the right time
requires effort?

71

(155)

The first-born of the forest,
a tree with twice the others' years,
whose roots are twisted
to the valley's contours
and whose leaves the
wind and frost have scarred,
is mocked by all
because its sides are bare
rather than loved
because its grain is fine;
when bark and skin all fall away
then only truth and reality
remain.

72

(10)

Some fifty metres tall
a heaven-born tree
                    is felled
and trimmed along its length
for planking;
                    the trunk-
timber
            sadly abandoned
in the sunless valley
                    gathers
as the years go by
fresh strength at its heart
as every day
the dry bark falls away
wanting only
                    a wise carpenter
to come and make of it
the very
            ridge-pole of his barn.

73

(46)

Who lives for ever?
                    Death's
a thing
          that balances things out;
this comely
                    six-foot fellow
is suddenly
                    a fistful of dry dust,
who'll see
                    no dawn sky breaking
over the Yellow Springs
                              of Acheron;
though the green grass
                              grows on
to a timely spring,
                    we go
to a place
          that breaks all hearts;
for ever
          with their sad music
the pine trees
                    sing us to our ends.

74

(22)

There is a saint
who lives on dew and haze
in a retreat
the vulgar cannot reach
to talk with whom
is freshness and delight
like autumn cool
on stifling summer days –
a dark stream ever rippling,
a tall pine with wind whispering –
to sit with whom
for half a day
is to forget
a century of regret.

75

(134)

Last night dreamed I had gone home;
saw my wife weaving at her loom
stop the shuttle as if in thought,
resume the weave but listlessly;
called her to turn and look at me;
startled, but did not know my face;
must be these many years apart have
changed the colour of my hair and beard.

76

(68)

The mountain-dweller's heart is small
and sear, ever sighing for time's
passing; as he with bitter labour
gathers herbs of life and simples
of longevity, how shall he
be immortal? This
enclosed garden
which the first clouds wrap,
this forest where the moon
is full and round – he
will not leave them; why not?
The beauty of the cassias
holds him back.

77

(67)

The mountains
are so very cold this year
as in years past; the snow
grips hard on every rolling range
and each dark forest
breathes its icy mist.
Though grass will grow again
after the season of young shoots,
trees will be bare again
before next autumn comes.
The traveller here is lost!
– seek how I will,
I cannot see the sky.

78

(69)

Man dwelling
        on the mountain way
where the clouds curl
and the mists swirl
picks a flower, thinks
of a lover long lost
to whom return would be hard
despite all longing –
heart dwelling
        on the irrevocable past,
old age has come
and nothing done;
how sad that all men
mock his waywardness!
He stands alone but
will keep faith.

79

(47)

Chestnut horse
    and coral whip
riding like mad
    along the Loyang road
quite in love
    with his own young beauty
does not believe in
    age and decay;
but the white hairs
    will grow
and the fresh complexion
    fade; look well
at that great mountain
    of noble graves –
there are no other
    "Isles of the Blessed".

80

(8)

Speaking on the subject
    of death and last rites
Chuang-tze claimed
    the whole cosmos for his coffin;
for my own predestined
    homecoming I need
a single sheet
    of bamboo planking;
let my dead flesh nourish
    the bright blue-fly,
I will not trouble
    the white crane by my passing;
let me say – as was said
    of the two noble brothers
who starved to death
    on Shouyang Hill –
that life was cheap and simple
    and death a pleasure.

81

(186)*

"Kanzan!
   your poems are rubbish!"
says my friend.
     "In my view,"
I reply,
   "like me, the ancient poets
were not ashamed of poverty."
At this he laughs out loud,
"As usual, you're right!
I'm rather tight
     for cash today;
how about
   helping me out?"

82

(253)

Since the creation of the heavens
and the earth, man has been
trapped between them. "Man!
stray witless!" says the earthly mist;
"Come to your senses!" howl the winds of heaven;
"Unhappy man!" says earth and sends him wealth;
"Intemperate!" says heaven, imposing poverty.
Thus men are rolled from side to side
like pebbles in a torrent; everything
depends upon the Lord Creator.

83

(62)

A jostling of court ladies
in the evening sun; a light
breeze rises till the whole
street is mad with perfume;
a palpitation of butterflies
in gold sewn on the hems
of skirts; on impudent coiffures
conjugal ducks sail by in jade;
ladies-in-waiting in tight gowns
of crimson silk; and last of all
in tunics of purple cotton
come the accompanying eunuchs
– a sorry sight, for one of them
has clearly lost his way;
his hair is white and his heart
can know no rest.

84

(61)

Girls in spring
in sweet array
gathered in
the sun-drenched
alley-way
regretful
that the day
is short,
shelter
beneath the trees
before the cold
breeze rises;
white horse
and harness
of yellow gold –
a youth comes by;
he should not be
too bold and
linger there
too long;
her husband
will find out.

85

(60)

Loyang's innumerable girls,
seen at their loveliest
in spring, go gathering
wayside flowers –
adornments for extravagant
coiffures;
       with
hair swept high and
nodding flowers they seem
provocatively gay;
illusory!
       for every one
will take her way
back to a blameless
husband and home.

86

(23)

"I come
            from the land of Kantan
a singing-girl
                        from a land of singing
famous for voices
                        well curved to the song
and for the sweet
                        quiet of its dwellings
and the authentic
                        antiquity of its odes
like the one
            I have just sung;
but I can see
                you are drunk, so please
do not talk
            of going home now
but stay on
            till the day is full
in the room
            where I sleep
on a silver bed
            all spread
with an embroidered
                        coverlet."

87

(292)

Above the flowers
a yellow nightingale
in lovely song –
and here
as fine as jade
a courtesan
upon her lute.
Two sound as one,
ecstatic harmonies
of love and youth.
But now
the flowers have faded
and the bird has gone;
in the autumn wind
her tears fall like rain.

88

(14)

Soft eyebrows
    like moths' wings,
pearl girdle,
    jewels jangling,
a cockatoo
    she darts from flower to flower,
beneath the moon
    strumming her mandolin,
and rules the town –
    long songs
that echo for three months,
    brief dances
that ten thousand
    come to view;
let her not think
    it will be always thus:
hibiscus flowers
    cannot stand the cold.

89

(146)

Be happy
as chance comes, for
time
will not wait life's
full
hundred years
nor even
thirty thousand days; our
world's
moment is brief
and money is not
the answer; see
in this connection
the last chapter of
the Classic of Filial Piety
for an exhaustive
exposition on
death's finality.

90

(25)

The intellectuals
cannot abide me;
                I
have no time for fools
for I am neither fool
                       nor
intellectual!
            From now on I'll
have done with all of you!
When night-time comes
I'll sing to the rising moon
and
      with the dawn
                 I'll dance
with the high white clouds –
                   or rather
close my mouth
and still my hands
sit quietly
and let the breeze dance
wanton
        through my hair.

91

(20)

A place to be at peace –
if that is what you want
then this cold mountain
is a constant surety;
                    a
light wind blows the dark
mysterious pines;
                    the sound
grows lovelier as the ear
                    draws close.
Here sits
        a freckle-headed fellow
mumbling the Classics
– Lao-tze and the Yellow Emperor
                    – ten years
without returning to the world
even the path he came by
                    is forgotten.

92

(2)

I choose to live
        where crag
mounts upon crag,
the birds' path beyond
man's imprint;
        the
precinct of my
        garden is
white cloud
        that winds
about dark rock.
How many years have I
been here?
        I cannot say, save
that innumerable springs
have passed
        to countless autumns.
You down there!
        living
your well-fed lives to
the beat of a dinner gong!
– your empty reputations
rouse no envy;
        all
your ways
are vain and profitless.

93

(226)

How pleasant is the Path
of imperturbable normality!
the ivy curls like smoke
around the hollow rocks;
free as the virgin landscape
my untroubled heart
soars to the companionship of clouds.
This mountain road does not
lead back into the world;
my mind is still – who
shall invade my realm?
I sit in my own night-time
on this bench of stone;
above Cold Mountain
climbs the unwavering moon.

94

(273)

One hears that the
    Emperor Wu of Han, no
less than the first
    Grand Monarch of Ch'in,
was greatly drawn
    to the occult arts and the
lifelong quest
    of earthly immortality. The
Golden Tower
    of the one has crumbled
and the other
    sickened and died on Sandy Hill.
Today two tombs
    remain, and two illustrious
names, both covered
    by the deathless grass.

95

(156)

A hairless grub
on Cold Mountain,
white-bodied,
dark-headed,
clutching two slim volumes –
one on the Way
and one on Virtue –
dwelling without facilities
of kitchen or cooker,
walking abroad without
a skirt or shirt,
but holding to the scimitar
of Wisdom
         and plotting
to break the pate
of brigand Anguish.

96

(16)

Dwelling beneath
    the blue-green crags my
garden is
    a luxury of weeds
where ivy crawls
    with newborn fingers and
old stones sit
    straight as pinnacles.
The fruit of trees
    I leave for monkey-
fodder and the
    pond-fish for white cranes
to eat, and read
    one or two volumes
of the writings
    of the saints, mumbling
their words aloud
    beneath the trees.

97

(49)

Since I first set my face
to this cold mountain hermitage
some thirty years have passed
and yesterday I visited old friends
and felt half of my lifetime
slipped into oblivion, and faded
as a slow-dying candle fades
and listless as a sluggish stream.
This morning once again facing
my solitary shadow, tears stole
unwittingly down both my cheeks.

98

(147)

Meditating alone, how my mind
                wanders, wanders!
Recalling the past, how my heart
                ponders, ponders
In the bosom of the mountain, the clouds
                spread and spread!
But at the valley mouth, the wind is
                dread, so dread!
Monkeys in the branches make the trees
                quiver, quiver!
Birds fly into the woods, their voices
                quaver, quaver!
Time presses and my beard is
                grey, so grey!
The years are running out and my life is
                dead, dead!

99

*(163)**

Since coming here
          to dwell
                    in this cold mountain
how many myriad
          aeons
              have vanished
fate-vanquished
          fled
              to the woods and streams
invisibly
      locked
          to an awareness of the
ground of things;
          no men
              tread these lone pinnacles
where the white cloud
          endlessly
              gathers and drifts apart;
the delicate grass
          declines
           into a couch;
the blue sky is
          a coverlet;
           and any stone is my carefree
pillow;
      heaven
          turns and earth
changes, and I
      revolve
          with them.

100

(190)

Whether there is
                or is not
an individual subject,
and whether this
                is I or not I?
and so on and so forth ...
                    I sink
into speculative reverie
                   almost
out of time
           as I sit
leaning against the crag
until the green grass
sprouts between my feet,
and on my head
the red dust settles;
suddenly I perceive
the village people come
and offer wine and cakes
to my departed ghost.

101

(3)

How pleasant is Kanzan's path!
with no track of horse or carriage
over linked valleys
with unremembered passes,
peak upon peak
of unknowable heights
where the dew
weeps on a thousand grasses
and the wind
moans to a single pine;
now at the point
where I falter in the way
my form asks my shadow:
Whence came we?

102

(9)

Men ask about Kanzan's path
but Kanzan says his road
is inaccessible,
summer skies
where the ice has not melted
and sunshine
where the mist hangs thick;
how will you draw close
to one like me when your heart
is not as my heart? If only
your heart were as my heart
you would reach the centre.

103

(256) *

The people of our times
are trying to track out
a path to the clouds
but the cloud-path is trackless –
high mountains
with many an abyss,
broad valleys   .
with little enough light,
blue peaks
with neither near nor far,
white clouds
of neither east nor west.
You wish to know
where that pathway lies?
It lies in utter emptiness.

104

(51)

My heart is like the autumn
moon melting its silver in
the limpid lake – what else
should I compare it to?
– declare it to me!

Envoi

105

(141)

A third-rate simpleton
who reads my verse
will fail to understand
and bluster his dissent;
a second-rate or
average man
will ponder it, and then
pronounce it excellent;
a first-rate sage
will laugh out loud
as soon as it is
put into his hand,
like Yoshu in the *ageless*
tale, cracking the cipher on an *ancient*
tomb, and laying bare the *wonderment*
that hides behind the meaningless.

106

(311)

A house
        that has my poems
has better reading
                than the
scriptures;
        write them out in style
on paper screens,
                and read them
once
    in a while.

Hanshan's place in history

Religious Verse in the East Asian Tradition

The traditions of East Asian literature deriving from China represent an impressive stretch of continuous literary consciousness, spanning about three thousand years into modern times. One of the most striking differences between this continuum and the time-span covered by Western literature is the relatively unimportant role played in it by religious literature. There are, of course, exceptions, and Hanshan is one of them. But to understand just how and why Hanshan is exceptional requires some background information on how the literary tradition developed in China, and how its values came to differ from those that are presumably more familiar to the reader of English.

It cannot be denied, for example, that poetry stemming from a religious background existed in early China, during the time of intellectual ferment that preceded the consolidation of the Chinese empire in 221 BCE under the First Emperor, the monarch whose terracotta army still astonishes the whole world. One good example would be "The Far Journey", a work translated (as noted below, in "Hanshan in translation") by Peter Hobson. An even more meticulous and fully annotated version published more recently by Paul Kroll brings out yet more clearly the rich mythological background, without an understanding of which the poem loses much of its meaning.[1] But lose its meaning it did, together with other similar works, by becoming associated with China's first named poet, Qu Yuan, who lived about 343–290 BCE. Qu Yuan was a statesman in a southern kingdom facing the advancing might of the powerful northwestern state that eventually brought the First Emperor to the throne of a unified China, but he was entirely unsuccessful in persuading his own monarch of the approaching danger. After penning a lengthy poem drawing on religious imagery to express his disillusion with the political world,

115

he eventually committed suicide by drowning – indeed, it is the search for his corpse that dragon-boat racers are supposed to be re-enacting annually.[2] Finding no vindication in his own life, and apparently without the comfort of feeling that he was vindicated in the eyes of any all-seeing divine power, the appeal of his impassioned verses was to the wise men of posterity, who would recognize his true worth in another age.

Strange as it may seem to suggest that this resulted in all early religious poetry being interpreted as political metaphor, the first point that should be offered in explanation is that the story of Qu Yuan encapsulated one of the deepest and most enduring problems for the Chinese poet. As a man of education, he expected his learning to be put at the disposal of society through government service; that notion had already been established by Confucius and his followers. But what if his qualities were not recognized? The persistently autocratic nature of the Chinese state, while ameliorated by some meritocratic features such as the eventual emergence of civil service examinations, still created a steady stream of articulate and educated people who believed that they deserved better. Suicide was deemed extreme (although it happened), and a retreat into the life of a hermit usually appealed as a reasonable compromise. But the striking example of Qu Yuan meant that even to become a hermit was to take a political step, and any subsequent religious elements in lifestyle or in literature tended to be read as a form of coded political message.[3]

In any case, especially after the unification of 221 BCE, politics (or rather the world of government) became so dominant in the life of the educated elite as to acquire almost a sanctity of its own. For while the political ambitions of the Greeks tended to centre on the society of the city, and orators like Demosthenes reserved some of their most savage rhetoric for empire-builders, Chinese from Confucius onwards (if not before) tended to idealize the rule of ancient sage-kings, so the realization of a unified empire – even a rather brutal one – was still for the majority of thinkers (apart from an anarchistic few) in some respects a dream come true. Both Confucians and followers of the First Emperor agreed, after all, that the perfect society could be created in this world, not deferred to any world to come. If anything, the occasional imperial obsession with becoming literally immortal reflected a desire to perpetuate residence in this world, rather than to transcend it. True, an interest in immortality could perhaps be combined with yearnings for an alternative to this life, but in literature at any rate it seems to have remained throughout the centuries of successful early imperial rule strictly at the level of metaphor.[4]

116

What eventually caused a shift in the situation was, of course, the decline and virtual collapse of imperial power in the second century CE, during the late Han dynasty. We are, of course, familiar with the notion of imperial decline and the rise of new religions from the early history of Christianity and its rivals in the Roman Empire, and it cannot be denied that certain parallels with the introduction of Buddhism in China do exist. But just as I have suggested that China's attitudes towards the very idea of empire were from the start different from those in the West, so, too, did the consequences of the collapse of empire affect Chinese religion in ways that cannot be exactly paralleled elsewhere. For so powerful had the hold of empire become on the imagination of China's inhabitants that the unseen world of the spirits was seen as a vast bureaucracy as well – indeed, this process seems to have got under way even before the triumph of the First Emperor.[5] As a result, when the Chinese lost their faith in the government of men and turned to the government of the gods, they tended to turn to a priesthood that claimed to serve this unseen bureaucracy, addressing to it not prayers of supplication so much as bureaucratic memorials. It was indeed spectacular rebellions on the part of groups inspired by such ideas that rocked the empire to the very point of collapse.

Despite the failure of the rebels themselves, in the longer term their efforts established in Chinese society an organized and literate form of religion, one that gathered to itself many of those elements in earlier culture which stressed relationships other than those between the individual and society so beloved by Confucius and so ruthlessly refashioned by the First Emperor – other relationships such as between the human and the spirit worlds, or between humankind and the impersonal world of nature. Texts embodying such interests had already attracted the label "Taoist" during the early period of empire, and in time that title was adopted by this new form of religion.[6] But the consequences for literature were complicated by a simultaneous, related and yet in some degree opposed shift in the culture of the educated elite. As attempts were made to restore political stability without reference to the outmoded ideology of earlier imperial rule, which had come to rely on the promotion of Confucius and his followers, texts that formerly were marginal became more central to the culture, whereas those that had been central were read in new, more open-ended ways. Poets found a new freedom of expression in verse using a five-word (and later a seven-word) line drawn from, and at first closely modelled on, folk poetry. The tradition started by Qu Yuan of using poetry to meditate on history and, if need be, to appeal to its verdict was certainly strengthened, but the values of the new culture remained at this formative stage predominantly secular – to my mind deliberately so, given the elite's experience of the rebellious forces that could be unleashed by religious belief.[7]

So although it is possible to trace the development of an indigenous, Taoist religious literature throughout subsequent centuries, religious themes were slow to emerge, and seem never to have become central to the literary tradition as it developed its role of evaluating the past and addressing the future. The oldest layers of Taoist materials going back to the turbulent times following the crisis of the second century CE include versified texts, and when evolved forms of Taoism began to penetrate elite circles, largely through dispossessed southern aristocrats, the gods communicated to them hymns whose rhymes reveal the divine use of a distinctive form of southern accent.[8] Such reassurance was just what was needed by families who had been displaced from local power after a further disaster in the early fourth century caused the court to abandon all of North China and flee to present-day Nanjing. Indeed, as time went by and a succession of southern regimes kept up resistance to a barbarized north, some of the descendants of this dispossessed nobility built on both literary skills and religious learning to achieve a fair measure of fame and even influence – the great Tao Hongjing (456–536) provides a case in point.[9] But with the exception of one or two poetic genres, such as accounts of flights through the heavens, the Taoist generally fulfilled a bureaucratic role in relation to his or her gods, whereas poetry for most educated men was an alternative to writing in the service of bureaucracy.[10]

Similar considerations apply to Buddhism and literature. One can point to Buddhist poetry in Chinese from a fairly early stage, since although the religion was evidently not much discussed by the elite at the time of the second-century crisis, the early fourth-century collapse so dented the cultural self-confidence of the Chinese and impressed upon them the lesson of impermanence that fervent belief might be found quite soon thereafter in the highest circles.[11] But it is Buddhist faith expressed through the rhetoric of the Chinese literary tradition, rather than a distinctive form of religious literature, and to my mind the tradition perpetuated values which were fundamentally inimical to basic Buddhist beliefs: how might one achieve the fame necessary to address posterity while maintaining perfect non-attachment to this world?[12] Of course, Buddhism had its own poetic traditions going back to India, and many early gems of Buddhist verse are preserved there. But Chinese poetry depends crucially on rhyme, and it proved no more possible to render verse in Indian languages into rhymed Chinese than it has generally proved possible to render Chinese verse into rhymed English. The result was translation into a form of "blank verse" alien enough to the Chinese literary tradition, and further distinguished by its lack of intertextual references within that tradition, something which frequently gives to the most innocent and ballad-like line of Chinese from the second century CE onwards a depth of meaning quite invisible on the surface. That said, the situation had altered significantly by the time that Hanshan wrote, and it is important to know how and why.

The Rise of Buddhist Verse in China

It is of course undeniable that Buddhism in China changed in many ways as a result of a long-term process of adapting to Chinese culture; however, the ongoing cultural synthesis involved did not take place painlessly, but rather as the result of strong and sometimes violent pressures. Thus for example the emergence of texts ostensibly of Indian origin but actually composed in China and featuring prominently Buddhist teachings adapted to Chinese circumstances may be seen in a number of cases against the background of persecution by rulers influenced by Taoism in North China in the middle of the fifth century.[13] In the case of Buddhist verse, a new era seems to have been ushered in by the fall of the Liang dynasty in the south. For that dynasty is dominated by the reign of its founder, Emperor Wu (r. 502–49), who is usually depicted in Chinese sources as the most lavish patron of the Buddhist religion that China ever saw. A closer study of his reign, however, shows that Wu inspired something rather different from unquestioning devotion: in fact, he seems to have manipulated both the Chinese cultural heritage and Buddhism to create a regime sustained by a system of dual and separate ideologies in which his own imperial role was central.[14] His demise at the hands of a rebel after a long and apparently successful reign, and the subsequent collapse of his dynasty, certainly left Buddhists bereft of a stable political environment favourable to themselves. In the longer term, however, it also underlined the need to integrate Buddhist and Chinese culture rather than to develop Wu's dual system further. After all, in the troubled times that enveloped China, both North and South, in the late sixth century, many no doubt felt that the Buddha had lived not only long ago but also far away, and that the learned clergy studying abstruse Indian doctrines in their lavishly endowed monasteries practised a religion with no message of any value to those unfortunates caught up in the turmoil of the here and now.[15]

The consequences of this pessimistic, sometimes apocalyptic mood were far-reaching and profound. But one of the most immediate was the rejection of the pursuit of literary glory by a well-regarded courtier of the doomed Liang dynasty, who entered on a religious life under the name Wangming (literally "Abandoning Fame").[16] He devoted himself thereafter not to the showy and highly allusive poetry of the elite (though the circles from which he came had in fact produced literary works on religious topics), but to simple verses which enunciated the basic ideas of Buddhism on this world of suffering and how to transcend it.[17] The success of this strategy is confirmed by the discovery of his verses among the manuscripts from the Dunhuang caves.[18] This substantial treasure-trove of texts, mainly copied out during the latter part of the first millennium, was discovered near the ancient trading town of Dunhuang, in the northwest of Gansu province where China proper meets Inner Asia, at the start of the twentieth century and was subsequently scattered by expeditions of collectors across the libraries and museums of the world. As scholars have gradually catalogued and published the texts, a rare opportunity has been granted to see beyond the literature that the elite chose to preserve as part of their tradition, and, since these new sources seem to be connected in particular with a monastic library, some sort of picture emerges of how Buddhism affected the daily lives of ordinary people.[19]

But these texts also confirm that stepping beyond the bounds of the elite tradition did quite literally mean abandoning personal fame, in that many poems which circulated among the people seem to have been attributed to notional authors regarded as sources of popular wisdom, with no attempt made to distinguish between true and false attributions. One such author, who seems to have been regarded even shortly after his lifetime as a manifestation of Maitreya, Buddha of the Future, was a religious leader of the Emperor Wu's time named Fu Xi. At least some of the verses attributed to him must be of a later date, since the transcriptions of Sanskrit words reflect a pronunciation later than the sixth century, and it may be that we possess nothing actually composed by this man himself.[20] But some of the arguments deployed by scholars against other poems attributed to him come across as slightly circular. If his verses include apparently anachronistic philosophical ideas associated with the new schools of Buddhism that emerged from the ferment of the late sixth century to consolidate that period's innovations in the more stable times that followed, surely we should not disallow the possibility that the founders of these schools drew on ideas and insights already present fragmentarily in earlier poetry in building their more elaborate philosophical systems.[21] Certainly the

120

Dunhuang manuscripts bear witness to the fact that doctrinal masters of this new epoch, the reunited empire of Sui (589–618) and Tang (618–907) dynasty China, did not hesitate to use verse as a means of getting their ideas across to a wider public – including in particular, it seems, Shenhui (684–758), the promoter of a new form of what we know as Zen, or in Chinese pronunciation Chan.[22] But the same materials also bear witness to a type of Buddhist verse, probably of seventh-century origin, somewhat distinct from that which popularized the doctrines of one particular school – a much simpler and more direct vernacular folk Buddhist genre attributed to one Wang Fanzhi, meaning "Wang the Devotee", a shadowy figure of whom we know practically nothing.[23]

Wang's work has a direct relevance to that of Hanshan: even if the totality of the surviving works under his name show a number of differences from that contained in the Hanshan corpus, one recent translator of the former has listed nine or ten cases of overlap between the two, so it would seem that at least some of the Hanshan poems were written in the knowledge of Wang's earlier efforts.[24] This presumes, of course, that Hanshan is not an even earlier figure, a problem which will be confronted below, but at least we have evidence for one other poet quoting Wang by name in the late eighth century, whereas there is no mention at all of Hanshan up to that point.[25] The poet in question was actually a Buddhist monk, Jiaoran, a figure of some importance not in the development of the type of Buddhist verse just discussed, but in the development of critical norms relating to the verse of the elite.[26] His reference to Wang is therefore, perhaps not surprisingly, something of a backhanded compliment: he is mentioned for his ability to "stun the ordinary person" – *épater les bourgeois*, perhaps. Jiaoran's writings show him to have been an arbiter on matters of technique in a tradition that prized considerable complexity, whereas his theoretical pronouncements on poetry and religion may appear to us somewhat disappointing.

For Jiaoran was actually descended from a very famous Southern aristocrat and poet named Xie Lingyun (385–433), who had a great reputation also as a Buddhist devotee. Jiaoran naturally mentions this, but only by asking rhetorically "How could it not be that his Buddhism helped" in imbuing his writing with greater insight?[27] As a theoretical statement this amounts to little more than saying that it takes a worried man to sing a worried song, but for all the devoutly Buddhist poets who had appeared between Xie's time and Jiaoran's, no one seems to have come up with any more profound conception of the link between Buddhism and the literary life. That is not to say that signs of a reorientation of the relationship between high culture and Buddhism is not discernible to a close reader of Jiaoran's own writings and those of his circle. Jiaoran mentions Chan/Zen with some frequency, while the cult of tea was also a concern of his associates. Nowadays we all know about Zen and the art of the tea ceremony, and, given Hanshan's reputation as a Zen poet, this might be thought an appropriate point to enlarge upon the whole question of the origins and development of Zen culture. But that would be to take Hanshan's Zen affiliation at face value. Certainly it cannot be ignored, but a description of Hanshan's cultural context requires also a few words about his name and his location before the topic is taken up once again.

Of Poetry and Mountains

Anyone who has already read Hanshan's poetry might be forgiven for wondering why I have said so much by way of background before making any attempt to assess the man and his ideas. After all, Hanshan is a brilliant communicator, even in translation, and one might think that he has enough to say in his verses to reveal a virtually complete picture of his life and times. Unfortunately, as we shall soon discover, reading his poetry as a record of his life presents one major (though not entirely insoluble) problem. Some further scene-setting is necessary, but we may at least start from one incontestable biographical point: his choice of pseudonym. This recurs frequently enough in the poems for us to feel sure that it cannot be the result of later editing, and the very phrase "Cold Mountain" does tell us something about the person hiding behind its anonymity. It tells us, for example, that for all the apparent overlaps with the verse of Wang Fanzhi, who seems to have been very much what one would think of as a folk intellectual, quite unconcerned with the culture of the elite, Hanshan harboured some modest aspirations of a conventional literary type.[28] For "mountain" is one of the most commonly used words in the elite poetry of the Tang dynasty. Concordances are gradually appearing to cover all of the approximately fifty thousand poems of this epoch, and from their appended analyses of word counts it is clear that poets for whom "mountain" is only among their top twenty most frequently used words are somewhat unusual. For most concordances published so far "mountain" is in the top ten or top five; for many it is simply the most commonly used substantive of all.[29]

Why should that be? At a guess, because poetry in China, from Qu Yuan onwards, was largely concerned with representing an alternative to service in the bureaucracy. Indeed, much of it in Tang times depicts a world not far removed from that of work. All the poems of convivial parties, of sending off colleagues, of visits in company to scenic places, reveal a world no more private than the one inhabited after office hours by the modern Japanese executive, still surrounded by his colleagues and a long way from his family. But the mountain represents a way out, a potential, ever present alternative, even if the vast majority of poets duly headed back to the office again. It occupied another space, a sacred space, culturally (and sometimes ethnically) distinct, as historians of Chinese religion are increasingly finding.[30] And most intriguingly of all, in the complementary interplay of different forces, yin and yang style, in the traditional culture of China, it did not have to constitute an absolute alternative. Between the day-tripper from the office and the monk in his mountain cell there existed a third way, the way of the "mountain man", *shanren*.

As this term occurs in our texts it would seem to indicate someone who lives on a mountain but is not a member of any religious community. Typically he might have acquired a certain degree of religious or occult learning, but without affiliating himself with any particular religion. Many educated persons of the period felt free to combine an interest in both Buddhist and Taoist ideas, and the "mountain men" extended this lack of clear religious identification to a semi-religious lifestyle.[31] At the popular level sectarian distinctions seem to have counted for even less: it is interesting to note, for example, that Wang Fanzhi's work is mentioned in a Dunhuang manuscript which turns out to be of Taoist provenance.[32] This willingness to mix ideas from different traditions is, of course, one of Hanshan's characteristics, too. But what would have been the point of retreat to a mountain, other than as a decisive break with the secular world?

In short, for someone who had no office job to go to, but for whom a religious commitment seemed too radical a rejection of a career, then many mountains offered the possibility of pursuing an "eremitic" lifestyle as a medium-term strategy. Acting the hermit was a good way of opening up employment opportunities, since declaring oneself a man of principle in this way increased one's value on the job market. Of course, it would not do to be too overt about this: one mountain conveniently situated not too far from court was stridently condemned by a leading Taoist priest as a "back door to office".[33] As a result of such cases, the lives of "mountain men" attracted explicit legal restraints: they were subject to supervision by the local authorities and were not allowed (no doubt for fear of the political repercussions) to amass large numbers of students.[34] But it is not difficult to find in Tang sources instances of men who lived, sometimes for many years, on famous mountains, only to take up government service in due course.[35] For one of the great attractions of such mountains was the presence of substantial religious communities, usually both Buddhist and Taoist, with richly stocked libraries which offered excellent opportunities for improving one's education. Unlike the medieval universities of the Western world, which in Britain at any rate occupy somewhat soggy areas where scholars might find refuge from the hearty barbarity of the feudal elite, China's mountains offered an environment for learning that was at once tranquil, bracing and aesthetically pleasing. And, what is more, in China one's chances of employment were improved by education.

The Tiantai Mountains where Hanshan made his home were very much a location of the "university" type, long famous for their association with Buddhism and also with legends of the immortals; one Buddhist monk now best known as a great astronomer had received his mathematical training at a monastery there.[36] It may be that there was already a spot there named "Cold Mountain" before our poet arrived, but it is equally possible that he chose this name for his dwelling as well as for himself. If so, then that would confirm the impression he gives of having acquired a substantial education before abandoning his career hopes. The "Bible and Shakespeare" which constituted the main source of allusions for educated Chinese of the time were the Confucian Classics and the Wenxuan: the latter work is a standard literary anthology compiled in the early sixth century, in which the phrase "Cold Mountain" occurs several times.[37] So it would not be an obscure choice for a name, and indeed we find that Jiaoran uses it as well.[38] By the second half of the eighth century, too, we find near the city of Suzhou a "Cold Mountain Monastery", mentioned in a poem of the period by Zhang Ji that was anthologized by the end of the century.[39] In fact this quatrain became such a firm favourite that "Cold Mountain" and Suzhou would have been as inextricably linked for later readers as were "Cold Mountain" and Tiantai.

However, if those scholars are right who, in accordance with the traditional sources, would place Hanshan at an earlier period within the Tang dynasty, then the occurrence of these references might reflect indirectly the early spread of the Hanshan legend. We must therefore leave off for the moment a consideration of broader questions of the development of religious poetry in China, and turn to discussing the date of Hanshan himself, and to the many problems that such discussion entails.

Who was Hanshan?

As an increasing number of translations of Hanshan's work have started to appear in European languages, scholars across the world have cast an increasingly critical eye at the information which has traditionally been preserved concerning him, and have reached conclusions which both refute and affirm the traditional picture in a rather complex way. Iriya Yoshitaka, upon whose work Peter Hobson drew, pointed to sources implying a date much later than the seventh-century one in the traditionally transmitted preface to the poems.[40] Wu Chi-yu, on the other hand, examined all the traditional sources and concluded that the date given in the preface could be made to fit with a specific Buddhist of the seventh century, though not everyone has agreed with him.[41] But the most important contribution to the dating of Hanshan's poems has been made by E.G. Pulleyblank, in a close examination of their rhyme schemes.[42]

Pulleyblank's study proves beyond doubt that Hanshan's poems could not all have been written by the same man at the same time. In China, as in England, rhymes changed over the course of time: we no longer rhyme "newly" and "July" as Sir John Suckling did in the seventeenth century, for example. Yet Hanshan, who in his language is a robustly vernacular poet rather than any sort of antiquarian, at times rhymes very conservatively – no later than the seventh century in Pulleyblank's judgement. Elsewhere, however, rhymes of a ninth-century type may be found, while the preface dating Hanshan to the seventh century turns out, on the basis of some verse at the end, to be even later – perhaps tenth-century in origin. Unfortunately, rhyme schemes cannot be used to assign all of the poems unambiguously into separate groups, because (in a similar fashion to English) some rhymes did not change over this time-span sufficiently for variations to show up. But several incontestable conclusions may be drawn from this discovery, the most obvious being that we are dealing not with a single author, but at best an original Hanshan and a second, "Deutero-Hanshan" who imitated him at a later date. It therefore becomes impossible to construct a picture of Hanshan as an individual on the basis of the corpus of poetry as a whole, although once the clearly later works have been identified (as they are in this selection) the reader will be able to discern differences in outlook between the earlier and later works.

Or so it would seem, for there is actually no evidence against the more radical conclusion that the poems were written by various hands over a span of time, and that what appear to be autobiographical references may be explained alternatively as falling well within the bounds of poetic convention – for example, the sort of false rustic persona that we also find in European literature. Is it only our own romantic individualism that prevents us from seeing behind the masks of convention a coterie of monks of the Tiantai mountains, detectable only by their penchant for including references to their distinctive philosophy in their verses?[43] Weighing up the conventions of another time and another culture is an almost impossible task, and it cannot be denied that at least some of the poems come across as "exercises", of the sort which could transcend the bounds of the tradition only in the hands of a master of conventions – and which here do not, though they possess a certain charm. But if there was nothing new, nothing individual at all, in the Hanshan poems, they would surely not have had the impact that they did, even given the cultural changes I shall attempt to describe, which arguably thrust them into the spotlight in a way that may well have surprised whoever was responsible for them.

It must also be said that some readers – myself included – feel instinctively uneasy with the earliness of the date offered by Pulleyblank. Robert Henricks, for example, maintains that even in the early part of the corpus there are allusions to the events of 756.[44] In that year a rebel general succeeded in turning the emperor out of his capital and forcing him to flee south-westward through the mountains to Sichuan, causing a dynastic near collapse and marking out a new age of protracted civil struggle and warlordism. It is possible to imagine Hanshan, as a man of humbler origin than those who had dominated government in less volatile times, trying to parlay his hard-won education into a civil service post during such an epoch, only to hit a glass ceiling at the first stage of the examinations because of a rustic country accent decades behind the sophisticated speech of the mandarins of the day. Disillusion and retreat were much in the air, and in the 760s and 770s a mountain was a safer place to be than most. To be fair, however, Pulleyblank appears to think that a conservative and rustic dialect difference cannot account for his rhymes, even if our current lack of knowledge of the complete picture of Chinese dialects at this time offers me some hope that this "romantic individualist" scenario might still just fit.[45]

There are, however, other indications pointing to the 760s or 770s. Some linguistic research would place the general pattern of Hanshan's grammar in the middle of the eighth century, though only on the untenable hypothesis of single authorship for the Hanshan corpus.[46] But, most intriguingly, the earliest external evidence (once the preface is discounted as late) for the date of Hanshan also explicitly puts him at this time, and this comes from a source whose significance has perhaps been under-valued: a compendium on Taoist immortals by the great Taoist priest and writer Du Guangting (850–933) which nowadays only exists in quotation. Its author describes Hanshan as an immortal evidently on the basis of information drawn from his earliest editor, a Taoist priest of the early eighth century named Xu Lingfu.[47] Xu himself was a well-known author, and one of his surviving works, composed in 825, is actually a description of the Tiantai Mountains where Hanshan made his home.[48] Puzzlingly, this work fails to mention Hanshan, but it is hard to be sure of the significance of this. First we should note that it survived to the present day only through a single manuscript preserved in Japan, and it may well be that this manuscript was incomplete.[49] Thirteenth-century commentary on a Tang poem, at any rate, would appear to quote a passage from Xu's record that is not (unless I am mistaken) in the present work.[50] Secondly, a reading of Xu's treatise suggests that descriptions of his editorial labours on behalf of unknown poets were probably not part of his agenda, since he stresses far more all connections between his mountains and the high and mighty, particularly emperors. Nor need we make much of the fact that a later Taoist hagiographer, taking up Du's story, refers to its subject as "Cold Cliff"; by the mid-twelfth-century date of this author the Buddhist associations of Hanshan may have been such as to encourage him to believe (or to seek to make others believe) that two different hermits were involved.[51]

It may be, of course, that Du Guangting made the whole story up to discomfort contemporary Buddhists, and attributed his information to Xu, a fellow disciple of his teacher's teacher. There is indirect evidence that the great Zen master Linji (perhaps better known as Rinzai), who died in 866, wrote some responses to Hanshan's poems, so it may be that Du was already countering a Zen claim on Hanshan.[52] But there is certainly evidence quite independent of Du Guangting, and hitherto apparently entirely overlooked, that testifies to a Taoist interest in Hanshan during the tenth century or earlier. This is in the form of a work on mystical alchemy still preserved in the Taoist canon under his name; since it is incorporated in a famous anthology of the early eleventh century the presumption must be that it dates at the latest to somewhat before that time.[53] Exactly how much earlier is a somewhat imponderable question: the text cites work in a similar vein by one Tao Zhi, who is supposed to have achieved immortality in 825, and so it is unlikely itself to be the composition of a recluse living in the late eighth century.[54] But its message is not necessarily irreconcilable with the remarks about alchemy found in the Hanshan corpus, since the text is not dealing with alchemy in a literal sense, but in the spiritual terms of the "internal alchemy" that was becoming increasingly popular at this time.[55]

Of course, this new information gets us no closer to solving the mystery of Hanshan: where even those much closer to his life in time and space were evidently unclear as to his identity, there is little hope that we will ever know who he was. Yet taking the Taoist materials seriously does tell us one or two useful things. The first is that at least by the time of Du Guangting, who specifically mentions Xu as compiling an edition of three hundred plus poems, the Hanshan corpus was more or less closed. As such scholars as Victor Mair have made clear, "three hundred plus" is, as a result of ancient precedents, an ideal number of items for a poetry collection.[56] The presumption has therefore been that the Deutero-Hanshan verses were added to the original core (itself a mere fragment of Hanshan's total output, if his own words are to be believed) in order to make up this number.[57] Since the makeweight poems are not conspicuously Taoist, the probability of Xu being Hanshan's first editor is actually quite low.

Secondly, however, it must surely be the case that the Taoists would not have tried to dispute Hanshan's legacy if he had initially been unambiguously a Zen poet. Bearing analogous cases of dispute at this period in mind, my own conclusion would be that Hanshan could be clearly identified with neither group.[58] This explains my introduction of the category of "mountain man" as the most appropriate background against which to understand Hanshan himself, despite the picture created by later legend. But, whether I am right or wrong, it cannot be denied that Hanshan's influence on later literature was exercised through his legendary image as a man of Zen. How and why that image came into existence is therefore an essential preliminary to any discussion of his place in the further history of religious verse in East Asia.

The Conversion of Hanshan

Zen was last mentioned above in connection with the monk poet Jiaoran in the late eighth century, and there, as earlier, no attempt was made to define the word. Nowadays, however, we all have some sense of what it means – or do we? It is, after all, just a label, as imprecise and slippery as any other. And without understanding its imprecision, its everyday ordinariness as an imperfect receptacle of meaning, we are unlikely to make much of its entanglement with literature. It means, as any standard East Asian dictionary of Buddhism will tell you, meditation, one of the three basic elements in all Buddhist practice. Since all Buddhists following the path of religious training undertake meditation, all practising Buddhists are Zen Buddhists, one might think. But all Christians in some sense affirm the importance of baptism, while not all Christians are Baptists. In other words, Zen has become a label for a particular sort of Buddhist because, like baptism, it became an issue. When and where did this happen?

The answer is: in China, during the period of doubt and uncertainty we have already described as having given rise to Buddhist verse. Just as Wangming and his contemporaries felt that the Buddhist message contained in translated texts was not getting across to the bulk of the Chinese population, so others feared that all literature transmitted from so long ago and far away was unlikely to help them in their religious predicament. Was there no other way of feeling in touch with the Buddha? Yes: for the practice of meditation, a skill not wholly describable in words, was still taught by masters whose training can be traced back through successive teachers to none other than the Buddha himself. If the ultimate message of Buddhism (which all agreed was a truth too cosmic to be captured in words) had been transmitted by such a lineage of masters, then China in the sixth or seventh century was as good a place and time to learn it as any other. That is why the so-called patriarchs of Zen, beginning with Bodhidharma, loom so large in East Asia from this time on.[59]

This message carried particularly interesting overtones in the world that began to emerge painfully after the disasters of 756 and the breakdown in civil order that (as we have speculated) may have driven Hanshan to his mountain. For a new form of the questioning mood found earlier in Buddhist circles now affected the Chinese literary and political elite, regardless of religious affiliation. Hitherto, and most clearly since the times of Emperor Wu of the Liang, educated men had been happy to compartmentalize their lives, expressing their undoubted religious piety, whether Buddhist or Taoist, only on set occasions and leaving religion largely to professional monks or priests. In the late eighth century, however, we find a new seriousness of purpose which groped towards the idea that life should be of a piece, not divided into different realms. This "Search for Unity", as it has been termed, has largely been characterized as promoting the emergence of Confucianism as a spiritual force, newly combining the values espoused by government with an interest in the inner dimension formerly left to the established religions to promote.[60]

But it can also be seen in the first stirrings amongst Jiaoran and his circle towards bridging the gap between the culture of the literati and that of Buddhism. Here there was one impediment above all others to the emergence of a Buddhist literary culture, and that was the Buddhist opposition to alcohol. For, as James Liu has made clear, the association between alcohol consumption and poetic composition in China was not, as in Britain, an occasional and perhaps mainly Celtic quirk, but a firmly established and in its way decorous part of social convention.[61] One obvious answer was the promotion of the cult of tea.[62] But Zen also had its uses: "meditation", after all, covered not only a process of training, but also an altered state of consciousness achievable through training and no doubt as conducive to poetic composition as one achieved through the use of alcohol. This, at any rate, seems to me to be the best explanation of the growth over the next five hundred years after Jiaoran of the analogous treatment of Zen and poetry to the point where it became a cliché widely accepted not only in Buddhist circles but also beyond.[63]

One of the Hanshan poems contained in this selection could be read as a comment on this idea. Poem 15 (no.285 in the total corpus) ends with the assertion that there is no "Zen" in the poet's song. Most commentators have read this to mean that the mysterious quality of "Zen"-ness is beyond words, and can be found only in reality, not description, which is like the image of the moon in a pool, not the real thing. But Zen as a term for the ineffable seems to me to be an extended usage not found in the earliest texts, and it may be that the message is more straightforward: this is just a poem, I did not write it in any altered state of consciousness. Such a reading, at any rate, seems to me more in harmony with Hanshan's emphasis on the everyday mind. It is, of course, true that by the eleventh century Zen had indeed turned into something different. As one visiting Korean remarked at that point, it had become not a matter of practice, but of talk, of a rhetoric, as we would say.[64]

That, too, was a development that made sense. The concept of lineage embodied in the stories of Bodhidharma amounted to a history that enabled those in the Zen tradition to forget history, to put the alien, Indian roots of Buddhism behind them.[65] If the sayings of any Zen master were as true a reflection of the Buddhist truth as any ancient Indian text, then it became possible to create a new Buddhist culture in China, in which poetry alluded not to an alien, Indian past but to the words and deeds of purely Chinese masters. By this stage, moreover, a purely Chinese Buddhist culture was much more necessary, for unity and stability had returned to China by 960; but whereas reunification under the Song dynasty did allow a new type of much more urban and prosperous society to develop in most of China, considerable portions of the north were left in the hands of non-Chinese peoples who upheld the much more cosmopolitan form of Buddhist culture that had originally prevailed in the

Tang. Not unnaturally, Song culture tended to be more self-consciously Chinese, more interested in its own ancient roots.[66] The revived form of Confucianism we have already noticed in the late eighth century obviously thrived under such circumstances, but Zen had already achieved enough of a cultural unification of its own to present an attractive alternative, as new research is beginning to discover.[67]

At what stage, then, was Hanshan incorporated into this Zen culture? The overall process of its emergence was evidently a slow one: recent work by Mark Halperin has underlined the extent to which even late Tang literati remained aloof from direct involvement in Buddhism, whereas their Song descendants were much more prepared to participate in doctrinal disputes and so forth.[68] Even the emergence of Zen was quite a lengthy process: the term "Zen school" does not seem to be used until the time of Zongmi in the mid-ninth century.[69] At the same time, Zongmi seems to be moving beyond the concern with lineage that dominates his predecessors to talk of Zen in broader cultural terms. He certainly outlines a sort of "High Zen", covering various groups related by descent from the early patriarchs. But at a lower level his conception of a "Broader Zen" extends to many famous Buddhists, and encompasses both Fu Xi and Wang Fanzhi, though neither could convincingly be associated with Bodhidharma's lineage in any way.[70] The former, together with Wangming, was to find a secure place in Zen compilations from the early eleventh century, although the latter was by then excluded in favour of Hanshan, and so was forgotten in the long term.[71] Zongmi's evidence, then, would seem to agree with the other indications we have already seen of a Zen interest in Hanshan developing in the mid to late ninth century, not without Taoist opposition.

As for the full legend, which turns him into a dishevelled monk, a fellow disciple with his companion Shide of the Zen master Fenggan, the information provided by Wu Chi-yu enables us to date the former figure at least to the start of the tenth century and the latter to its end.[72] Once completed, this conversion to Buddhism was to allow Hanshan to travel to realms which for all his wanderings he cannot even have dreamed of. We may scour the writings of Song Confucian scholars to find Hanshan's poems only mentioned in passing in unguarded moments, and the literature of poetic criticism too seems not to have found his work worthy of discussion.[73] But to take these materials as any indication of his influence is surely to miss the point. For Hanshan did not go the way of Wang Fanzhi and sink into obscurity: quite the reverse, as we shall see.

The Legacy of Hanshan

It is possible to pick up, in texts of Buddhist provenance, allusions to the fully developed legend of Hanshan as presented in the preface of his poems shortly after it is first cited in the late tenth century, suggesting that the information therein rapidly became common property, just as his poetry did.[74] But although in the next couple of centuries Hanshan and his work were clearly known – and not just in Zen circles – we have to wait until the thirteenth century for a visible rise in his popularity. For it is to this period that all the earliest painted images of Hanshan, by himself or with Shide, would seem to belong, though there may be earlier literary references to such works that I have missed.[75] And again, while examples can be traced back to the eleventh century, it is to the fourteenth century that we owe the first entire collection of overtly "Hanshan style" poems, shadowing their originals verse for verse, by the monk Fanqi (1296–1370).[76]

The reasons for this are not far to seek. Eremitism was in the air, even in Confucian circles, following the collapse of China's first experiment in cultural self-sufficiency in the face of Mongol invasions.[77] And although the Mongols were in their own violent fashion remarkably cosmopolitan, as ready to promote Buddhism as Christianity or Taoism, many Zen monks by now felt a closer identification with their culture than with any transcultural religious heritage, and so followed the example of their Confucian compatriots.[78] But before leaving the Mongol period, it is worth tracing the eventual fate of Fanqi's work. It has sometimes been asserted that the Hanshan corpus never became part of any government-sponsored Buddhist canonical collection, and in the strictest sense that is true. Even as diluted by the work of Deutero-Hanshan, the work of the original bearer of the name shows too many signs of the intellectual independence of the individual "mountain man" to pass as straightfor-wardly orthodox by Buddhist standards.[79] In modern times the 1579 "Wang Zongmu" edition of Hanshan's works has been inserted into a reprint of the privately sponsored Jingshan Canon of the sixteenth to eighteenth centuries; but comparison with catalogues of the original version of this canon shows this to have resulted from twentieth-century editorial intervention.[80]

The Jingshan Canon did however print in 1673 the entire corpus of Hanshan's poems as cocooned within the safe orthodoxy of Fanqi's imitations, further enveloped in another series of later imitations by a seventeenth-century monk.[81] In the eighteenth century, moreover, the

Manchu Yongzheng emperor, in sponsoring a more lavishly produced but narrowly conceived Chinese Buddhist canon evidently designed to displace the privately sponsored efforts of his subjects, also included Hanshan in the canon through the inclusion of his own anthology of Zen literature, which he had compiled in 1733. His approach, however, shows a more autocratic touch, since he selected for inclusion only about 130 poems, not many more than are included here.[82] But at least that selection, and the imperial preface attached, shows that this non-Chinese emperor must be given credit for having read the whole collection with some discrimination.[83]

But, to return from the Manchu invaders to the time of their Mongol predecessors, some Chinese Zen masters preferred flight overseas to Mongol domination. Among those who moved to Japan were many who, inspired by Xutang Zhiyu (1185–1269), felt a particular affinity for Hanshan.[84] It is no surprise, therefore, to find his popularity increasing in Japan at this time also, for it is possible that his poems were imported to Japan as early as the eleventh century; they were certainly there in the twelfth.[85] But although circumstantial reasons have been put forward for supposing that the Japanese Buddhist poet Saigyō (1118–90) was influenced by Hanshan's example, it is not until stronger Zen links with China develop from the thirteenth century onward that Hanshan's impact becomes undeniable.[86]

Indeed, for some monks of the so-called Gozan or Five Mountains, the monastic centres from which the newly imported Zen cultural package of religion and the arts started to be disseminated, the links with Hanshan were quite direct.[87] When Mongol relations with China in due course allowed, some made their own visits to China, so we find Tengan Ekō (1273–1335) writing of Hanshan on the basis of a personal visit to the Tiantai Mountains.[88] But even those who never went to China were evidently familiar with his poetry, and in their attempts at writing Zen verse in Chinese one can detect subtler (and perhaps even indirect) influences, to do with tone and subject matter. For example, cat poems are scarcely known in the verse of the Tang literati; the following lines by Hanshan (not translated by Peter Hobson) are almost the first on record to mention this frequent companion of monks and hermits:

Since the tabby cat died,
The rats besiege my food supplies.[89]

Yet cat verses among the Gozan poets (perhaps taking their tip from their Chinese masters, rather than direct from Hanshan) are not hard to find, and one has even been translated into English.[90]

Nor was this influence in the long run confined purely to Japanese literature written in Chinese. The seventeenth-century haiku, for example, is normally regarded as an essentially Japanese type of poetry, and certainly since the Tokugawa regime of 1603–1867 regulated contact with China quite carefully, no further direct inspiration from the Tiantai Mountains was available to Japanese. Even so, Matsuo Bashō (1644–94), the great proponent of the art of writing haiku, specifically acknowledged the debt he owed to Hanshan, and even inscribed one of his pieces on a portrait of his hero.[91] And Hakuin Ekaku (1686–1768), most famous of Japan's later Zen masters, carried his own tribute to the point of researching a detailed commentary on Hanshan's verse, as did several other Japanese monks of the age.[92] At the same time the tradition of composing Buddhist verse in Chinese did not die out, so that even in the early nineteenth century poets like Ryōkan (1758–1831) still express a great admiration for Hanshan.[93] Finally, when Japanese were able to travel freely to China again, the great Japanese politician Itō Hirobumi is said to have discharged the cultural debt he felt was owed to Hanshan by donating a bell in 1905 to the Hanshan Monastery near Suzhou.[94] Modern Sino-Japanese amity, unfortunately, was not irreversibly secured by this, and according to Jiang Yi (1903–77) the bell was repatriated to Japan during World War II.[95]

Thus, it may be seen that a sort of Hanshan tourism industry was gradually coming into being, based on a place more accessible than the chilly peaks of the Tiantai range. The earliest source linking Hanshan the poet with the monastery in Zhang Ji's poem dates back no further than the beginning of the fifteenth century, to judge from the researches of Wu Chi-yu.[96] By the late nineteenth century, however, as one observer noted, for all the delights of its scenery Tiantai attracted very few travellers.[97] Today, it seems, the Hanshan Monastery presses home its advantage, selling souvenirs to tourists of every kind.[98]

But although the tourism of today may be more international than ever before, an appreciation of Hanshan outside China has never been the preserve of the Japanese alone. True, the Gozan monks reprinted his works from Chinese editions, but another important early reprint comes from fourteenth-century Korea.[99] As for Vietnam, a source of about the same period affirms that two Zen adepts of that country were in fact reincarnations of Hanshan and Shide.[100] No doubt such thoughts were stimulated by references to incarnation in the materials on which the Hanshan legends are based, for back in China the imitators of Hanshan included in the Jingshan Canon, and the patron of the Wang Zongmu edition, are also awarded the accolade of being deemed reincarnations of the man himself.[101] But here the Vietnamese seem to have anticipated a remarkable twentieth-century phenomenon. Sir Reginald Johnston (1874–1938), one-time tutor to the last emperor of China, governor of the British China colony of Weihaiwei, and finally a most reluctant Professor of Chinese at the School of Oriental and African Studies in the University of London, is reported to have recounted in a lecture replete with references to Hanshan in Chinese and Japanese art how he, too, was mistaken for Hanshan redivivus.[102] And it has been pointed out that Jack Kerouac, in *The Dharma Bums* (1958) evidently viewed Gary Snyder, the pioneer translator of Hanshan, in much the same light.[103]

Now other Chinese poets have won international renown, but no other Chinese poet has induced quite such a reaction as this. And perhaps that makes a nonsense of any attempt to confine Hanshan to a particular place in history. He seems by these accounts determined to jump out of history – this despite his poetry having much less of an eye for posterity than that of any of his peers, or indeed betters. Any account of Hanshan in history must finally confront the quite remarkable paradox of Hanshan himself.

On Cold Mountain

Whoever Hanshan was, he seems to have succeeded – doubtless without the faintest intention of doing so – in becoming a perennial outsider figure throughout a far wider world than he could ever survey from his mountain hermitage. And this his poetry achieved, as he himself noted, by breaking every rule in the book. True, there are enough allusions to earlier writings in his works to show that he belonged to the fringes of literati culture, but at the same time his use of colloquialisms is markedly greater than his peers seem to have permitted themselves. He appears to be writing not so much in a style as a register all his own, and it is this very individuality as much as any verbal echoes which win him in later times one or two notices from critics comparing him to Qu Yuan or to his legendary predecessor, the Madman of Chu.[104]

It may be appreciated therefore that it was not the mainstream of literati culture that sustained an interest in Hanshan, but a subculture (albeit a widespread one) of educated Zen enthusiasts. That subculture evidently could not save Wang Fanzhi from oblivion after about five hundred years, until the accidental recovery of his writings from the Dunhuang manuscripts.[105] Exactly why that was we can only guess: perhaps no picturesque legend gathered around Wang, and the greater reliance of his verse on an increasingly outdated colloquial style may have told against him. One notes, for instance, that the records of Fu Xi's deeds were rewritten in the twelfth century to eliminate their ancient colloquialisms and make them fit for an increasingly sophisticated Zen culture.[106]

Conversely, Hanshan seems if anything to have gained in stature over the centuries, in the same way as the poets more central to the literati tradition, like Du Fu (712–70), who emerged as indubitable classics over more than a millennium of the constant evaluation of literary critics.[107] Yet despite the references to him in Zen verse, Hanshan does not seem to owe his survival to having become, through allusion or quotation, part of the intertextual fabric from which the mainstream tradition was fashioned, as Du Fu did. More typically his poetry was perpetuated, as we have seen, through imitation. This happened in the mainstream, too: Zhang Ji, author of the Cold Mountain Monastery poem, was an ardent emulator of Du Fu. But in Hanshan's case wholesale imitation took place, and this is perhaps a clue to the nature of his impact.

For despite his fumbling attempts to write like a true Tang poet, Hanshan was just too marginal to succeed. This, perhaps accidentally, created one very startling effect – one that prompted emulation, rather than allusion. To his contemporaries, becoming a hermit was (as tradition dictated) an issue, and they could not but write of eremitism that way. To the unfortunate Hanshan it was a cold, hard fact, just as much as a cat was a cat and a rat a rat. It is precisely when he is distracted from the literati tradition by the realities of his existence that his poetic gaze becomes utterly individual: clear, direct and even startling. What is more, this clarity of vision prevents his religious insights from becoming mere preaching – something which the religious poet Deutero-Hanshan obviously envied, but did not always succeed in duplicating.

For Nishitani Keiji is probably right: if there is a touch of Zen in the genuine Hanshan, it is not because he was a follower of that movement.[108] Rather, the likelihood is that the movement followed him and Zen underwent a touch of Hanshan. There is nothing to prevent us supposing, for example, that Zen incorporated his notion of the "everyday mind" – the Path of imperturbable normality, as Peter Hobson has it – from poetry into their doctrine in the same way as it seems possible that Fu Xi's poetic insights (if they were his) may have stimulated later, more systematic philosophical thought. True, this emphasis on the "everyday mind" was not perhaps entirely beneficial for subsequent Zen verse. Although "Zen verse" suggests writing infused with the insights of enlightenment, we must accept (as Nguyen explicitly does for Vietnamese Zen poetry) that much of it was just as conventional as mainstream, elite verse, though in another way.[109] Simplicity and directness, especially when allied to the predictability of a structured monastic environment rather than the alarming vicissitudes of a solitary hermit life, often produced at best mere charm, and at the worst pointless insipidity. But Hanshan's verse remained, and remains, a challenge.

On Cold Mountain, more than twelve centuries ago, a man whose name we will never know somehow learned, even if painfully and partially, to be himself. And not only was the poetic language he wrote in affected ever after, wherever it was used; now cultures incapable of reading his original words have, thanks to translators like Peter Hobson, been touched by his spirit. And who can tell how far the way to Cold Mountain will yet unfold through the centuries to come?

1. Paul Kroll, "On 'Far Roaming'", *Journal of the American Oriental Society* 116.4 (1996), pp.653–69.
2. The entire corpus of this poetry, together with a discussion of its actual and legendary origins, may be found in David Hawkes, *The Songs of the South: An Anthology of Ancient Chinese Poems by Qu Yuan and Other Poets* (Harmondsworth: Penguin Books, 1985).
3. An excellent study of the meaning of Qu Yuan for later Chinese culture may be found in Laurence A. Schneider, *A Madman of Ch'u: The Chinese Myth of Loyalty and Dissent* (Berkeley: University of California Press, 1980).
4. An essay establishing this point may be found by Donald Holzman, "Immortality Seeking in Early Chinese Poetry", the first study reprinted in his *Immortals, Festivals and Poetry in Medieval China* (Aldershot: Ashgate, 1998), from W.J. Peterson, A.H. Plaks and Y.-s. Yu, *The Power of Culture: Studies in Chinese Cultural History* (Shatin, NT, Hong Kong: The Chinese University Press, 1994), pp.103–18.
5. Evidence for this is presented in Donald Harper, "Resurrection in Warring States Popular Religion", *Taoist Resources* 5.2 (Dec 1994), pp.13–28, which article also introduces the research of Anna Seidel, who was primarily responsible for uncovering the situation in the second century CE.
6. The account of Taoism given here may well be unfamiliar to many readers, since it is based on more recent scholarship, which is not yet widely known. See, however, Isabelle Robinet, *Taoism: The Growth of a Religion* (Stanford: Stanford University Press, 1997).
7. A recent attempt at delineating the new culture of this period has been made by Christopher Leigh Connery, *The Empire of the Text: Writing and Authority in Early Imperial China* (Lanham, MD: Rowman and Littlefield, 1998): to my mind this study, by adopting the standpoint of the elite creators of literature, ignores the impact of alternative textualities which shaped their response. The various studies of Donald Holzman, including the volume listed above (n. 4), do however treat literary developments with much more of an eye for the religious background.
8. The aristocrats were several generations earlier colonials from the north, so their dialect was not southern by origin. On the poetry of the gods, see Terence Craig Russell, "Songs of the Immortals: The Poetry of the Chen-kao" (Ph.D. dissertation, Australian National University, Canberra, 1986).
9. Part of his achievement may be gauged from Michel Strickmann, "On the Alchemy of T'ao Hung-ching", in *Facets of Taoism*, ed. Holmes Welch and Anna Seidel (New Haven: Yale University Press, 1979), pp.123–92.

10. No overall account of Taoist literature within the Chinese literary tradition exists in English, though one may point to pioneering Chinese attempts such as Zhan Shizhuang, *Daojiao wenxue shi* (Shanghai: Shanghai Wenyi chubanshe, 1992).

11. For one early example that has been closely studied, see Richard Mather, "The Mystical Ascent of the T'ien-t'ai Mountains: Sun Cho's 'Yu T'ien-t'ai-shan Fu'", *Monumenta serica* 20 (1961), pp.226–45. This is technically a piece of what sinologists term rhyme-prose rather than poetry, but this genre tended to support the same values as poetry, and the piece is in any case interesting as an early description of the numinous environment later inhabited by Hanshan himself.

12. I have tried to explore this problem from a slightly different angle in "Exploratory Observations on some Weeping Pilgrims", in *The Buddhist Forum*, i, ed. T. Skorupski (London: School of Oriental and African Studies, University of London, 1990), pp.99–110.

13. Note for example Whalen Lai, "The Earliest Folk Buddhist Religion in China: T'i-wei Po-li Ching and its Historical Significance", in David W. Chappell, *Buddhist and Taoist Practice in Medieval Chinese Society* (Honolulu: University of Hawaii Press, 1987), pp.11–35.

14. A recent doctoral thesis, Andreas E. Janousch, "The Reform of Imperial Ritual During the Reign of Emperor Wu of the Liang Dynasty (502–549)" (University of Cambridge, 1998), presents a far more complex and interesting picture of the emperor than has hitherto been available.

15. Something of a flavour of the age and the concerns of Buddhists at this time may be found in Paul Magnin, *La Vie et l'oeuvre de Huisi (515–577)* (Paris: École Française de l'Extrême-Orient, 1979).

16. There is also a possibility that he intended his name to be read Wuming, meaning "Anonymous", a sobriquet that has stymied some anthologists. I have not come across any evidence to clarify this point, and it may even be that the ambiguity was deliberate.

17. One of his pieces is anthologized by Paul Demiéville on pp.21–2 of his *Poèmes chinois d'avant la mort* (Paris: L'Asiathèque, 1984).

18. For Wangming's verses at Dunhuang, see the article by Chen Zulong in *Tonkō to Chūgoku Bukkyō*, ed. Makita Tairyō and Fukui Fumimasa (Tokyo: Daito shuppansha, 1984), pp.471–99: the survey of research on the first two pages points to one study proving that his works circulated as far afield as seventh-century Japan. Note also Tanaka Ryōshō, *Tonkō zenshū bunken no kenkyū* (Tokyo: Daito shuppansha, 1984), pp.285–91, and pp.889–92 of the work by Xiang Chu cited in n.23 below.

19. For a summary of these sources and their value, see D.C. Twitchett, "Chinese Social History from the Seventh to the Tenth Centuries: The Tun-huang Documents and their Implications", *Past and Present* 35 (1966), pp.28–53.

20. See R.E. Emmerick and E.G. Pulleyblank, *A Chinese Text in Central Asian Brahmi Script* (Rome: Istituto Italiano per Medio ed Estremo Oriente, 1993), p.14. Fu Xi and his writings are also dealt with in the article by Chen cited in n.18, while the main source on his life is translated in Hsiao Bea-hui (religious name: Ven. Dawyuh), "Two Images of Maitreya: Fu Hsi and Pu-tai Ho-shang" (Ph.D. dissertation, University of London, 1995).

21. For a summary of the complex problems surrounding Fu's most famous composition and its relationship to works by other writers, see Tanaka's monograph cited in n.18 above, pp.313–34. The first scholar to point out the links between this piece and Tiantai Buddhism was Sekiguchi Shindai, in his *Daruma Daishi no kenkyū* (Tokyo: Shunjusha, 1969), pp.370–71.

22. Ren Bantang, in his remarkable masterpiece *Dunhuang geci zongbian* (Shanghai: Shanghai guji chubanshe, 1987), p.1425, accepts Dunhuang lyrics attributed to Shen-hui as genuine: he can hardly be accused of bias in favour of Buddhist masters, as his

republication of a distinctly hostile article on Buddhist verse by Long Hui on pp.1801–18 of the same work demonstrates.

23. Xiang Chu, *Wang Fanzhi shi jiaozhu* (Shanghai: Shanghai guji chubanshe, 1991), pp.906–26, carefully appraises what scraps of early evidence we have.

24. P. Demiéville, *L'Oeuvre de Wang le Zélateur* (Paris: Collège de France, Institut des Hautes Études Chinoises, 1982), p.876, gives a list of these overlaps in the index to his French translation of most of the surviving corpus of Wang's work. For some sample English translations, see Wu-chi Liu and Irving Yucheng Lo, eds., *Sunflower Splendor: Three Thousand Years of Chinese Poetry* (New York: Anchor Press, 1975), pp.83–84, by Eugene Eoyang.

25. Demiéville, *Wang le Zélateur*, pp.561–63.

26. The best brief summary of Jiaoran and his work is in Stephen Owen, *The Great Age of Chinese Poetry: The High T'ang* (New Haven: Yale University Press, 1981), pp.287–95.

27. In his *Shishi*, pp.29–30, as reprinted in He Wenyuan, *Lidai shihua* (Beijing: Zhonghua shuju, 1981), pp.26–36. The Wang Fanzhi quotation is on p.32; interestingly, Jiaoran traces back such verse to the "madman of Ch'u" from whom Schneider's book on Qu Yuan (n.3 above) takes its title.

28. A recent article comparing the two is Lu Yongfeng, "Wang Fanzhi shi, Hanshan shi bijiao yanjiu", *Sichuan daxue xuebao (zhexue, shehui kexue)*, 1999.1, pp.110–13. My thanks to my student Shi Zhenjing for supplying me with a copy of this article.

29. Just to cite a couple of examples, for Wang Wei, "mountain" comes second in his frequency list, after "man", according to Chen Kang and others, comp., *Quan Tang shi suoyin: Wang Wei juan* (Beijing: Zhonghua shuju, 1992), p.426; for Meng Haojan, "mountain" comes first, ahead of "man", in Chen Kang and others, comp., *Quan Tang shi suoyin: Meng haoran juan* (Beijing: Zhonghua shuju, 1992), p.282.

30. For some interesting remarks on the mountains as a potential home for alternative societies, see Glen Dudbridge, *Religious Experience and Lay Society in T'ang China* (Cambridge: Cambridge University Press, 1995), pp.76–85. For further references to research on the religious role of mountains, see my remarks in the introduction to *Writing Sacred Lives: Biography and Religion in China and Tibet*, ed. Ben Penny (Richmond, Surrey: Curzon, forthcoming).

31. Best known to the history of Chinese religious thought is Mountain Man Shi (Shi shanren), who posed ten questions on religious progress to the great Buddhist thinker Zongmi: see Peter N. Gregory, *Tsung-mi and the Sinification of Buddhism* (Princeton: Princeton University Press, 1991), p.83.

32. Xiang Chu, *Wang Fanzhi shi jiaozhu*, pp.912–18.

33. For this anecdote, see Ute Engelhardt, *Die klassische Tradition der Qi-Übungen (Qigong)* (Stuttgart: Franz Steiner, 1987), pp.48–49.

34. This according to a regulation dated to 702 included on the Dunhuang manuscript Stein no.1344.

35. For Hou Kao and Li Po (773–831), two such cases encountered in the course of my own earlier research, see T. H. Barrett, *Li Ao: Buddhist, Taoist or Neo-Confucian?* (Oxford: Oxford University Press, 1992), p.73; one might add also the chief minister Li Mi (722–89), mentioned on p.82. The "mountain men" of today, given the modern political situation, are, of course, true hermits without political ambition, but they still exist: see Bill Porter, *Road to Heaven: Encounters with Chinese Hermits* (London: Rider, 1994); readers of Hanshan may like to know that this work reveals Bill Porter and the translator Red Pine to be one and the same.

36. For the conception of the mountains as universities, and for Tiantai and the mathematical education of the monk Yixing in particular, see my remarks on p.429 of "Science and Religion in Medieval China: Some Comments on Recently Published

Work by Nathan Sivin", *Journal of the Royal Asiatic Society*, 3rd series, 8.3 (Nov 1998), pp.423–30.

37. Shiba Rokurō, ed., *Monzen sakuin* (Kyoto: Jimbun kagaku kenkyūsho, 1959), p.1273.

38. Owen, *Great Age of Chinese Poetry*, p.291.

39. Fu Xuancong, *Tangdai shiren congkao* (Beijing: Zhonghua shuju, 1980), pp.209–19 (especially the last four pages), covers Zhang, his poem, and his anthology appearance.

40. Iriya Yoshitaka, *Kanzanshi* (Tokyo: Iwanami, 1958), pp.7–10.

41. Wu Chi-yu, "A Study of Han-shan", *T'oung pao* 45.4–5 (1957), pp.392–450.

42. E.G. Pulleyblank, "Linguistic Evidence for the Date of Han-shan", in *Studies in Chinese Poetry and Poetics*, ed. Ronald Miao (San Francisco: Chinese Materials Center, 1978), pp.163–95.

43. Such a possibility is argued with detailed evidence from the poems in a review of the Henricks translation by Stephen R. Bokenkamp in *Chinese Literature: Essays, Articles and Reviews* 3.3 (1991), pp.619–24.

44. Robert G. Henricks, *The Poetry of Han-shan: A Complete, Annotated Translation of Cold Mountain* (Albany, N.Y.: State University of New York Press, 1990), p.7.

45. Pulleyblank, "Linguistic Evidence," pp.165 and 167 (but not on p.169), seems to treat "north" and "south" as homogeneous dialect areas for writers of poetry, and also to take what could be literary references to the old capital cities of the north as based on first-hand experience.

46. Qian Xuelie, "Hanshan shi yufa chutan," *Yuyan jiaoxue yu yanjiu*, 1982, 2, pp.109–26. Qian has subsequently published an edition and study of Hanshan, which unfortunately I have not had available to me.

47. Wu, "Study," pp.415–16, translates Du's evidence in full.

48. For Xu, see Franciscus Verellen, *Du Guangting (850–933): Taoïste de cour à la fin de la Chine médiévale* (Paris: Collège de France, Institut des Hautes Études Supérieures, 1989), pp.21–2.

49. Note p.338 of P. Pelliot, "Le Kou Yi Ts'ong Chou," *Bulletin de l'École Française de l'Extrème-Orient* 4 (1902), pp.315–40.

50. The commentary in Li Bai, *Li Taibai quanji* 21 (Beijing: Zhonghua shuju, 1977), p.971, which I assume to date back in origin to the Mongol period, quotes a portion of the *Tiantaishan ji* that is in the current text, and then a text by Shenyong that is not in the current text but which I take to be as cited from the same source (it seems unlikely to have survived so long independently). Even if these assumptions are wrong, Verellen, *Du*, p.22, notes another very surprising absence from Xu's text.

51. Wu, "Study," p.395, n.3.

52. Rinzai's work is mentioned twice in a late tenth-century source: see Henricks, *Han-shan*, p.25, n.37. On the date of Rinzai's death, I follow the arguments in Yanagida Seizan, "The Life of Lin-chi I-hsüan," *Eastern Buddhist* 5.2 (1972), pp.70–94.

53. Ren Jiyu, ed., *Daozang tiyao* (Shanghai: Guji chubanshe, 1991), pp.700–701, provides an overview of this text; for its incorporation into the well-known *Yunji qiqian* anthology, see K. M. Schipper, ed., *Index du Yunji qiqian* (Paris: École Française de l'Extrème-Orient, 1981), p.xlix.

54. Ren, *Daozang tiyao*, pp.188 and 686–87, surveys the works of Tao and gives the source of the date.

55. The best explanation of the tradition of mystical alchemy in question may be found in Fabrizio Pregadio, *Zhouyi cantong qi* (Venice: Cafoscarina, 1996); Tao is cited on p.39.

56. Victor Mair, "Script and Word in Medieval Vernacular Sinitic," *Journal of the American Oriental Society* 112.2 (1992), pp.269–78.

57. For Hanshan's own count of his output (itself a suspiciously round number) see poem no.270, Henricks, *Han-shan*, p.367. Clearly, a poet who by all accounts (including this

one) left his poems on the rocks for others to find was playing fast and loose from the start with his relationship with posterity.

58. For a study of a somewhat similar case, with references to other parallels, see chapter 2 of Barrett, *Li Ao*; one or two details in this chapter have been corrected in a review by Oliver Moore in the *Journal of the Royal Asiatic Society*.

59. This interpretation is further explored in T.H. Barrett, "Kill the Patriarchs!", in *The Buddhist Forum*, i, ed. T. Skorupski (London: School of Oriental and African Studies, University of London, 1990), pp.87–97.

60. The entire trend is seen through one famous example in Charles Hartman, *Han Yü and the T'ang Search for Unity* (Princeton: Princeton University Press, 1986), though it has also been studied by others, notably David McMullen.

61. James J.Y. Liu, *The Art of Chinese Poetry* (Chicago: University of Chicago Press, 1962), pp.58–60, who however defends Chinese poets against any assumption that they were habitual drunkards.

62. Marco Ceresa, *La scoperta dell'acqua calda* (Milan: Leonardo, 1993), provides a short but lively introduction to the relevant sources on this momentous cultural shift.

63. Stephen Owen, *Readings in Chinese Literary Thought* (Cambridge, MA: Harvard University Press, 1992), p.393 and p.626 n.9, gives the necessary secondary sources to trace the links; I regret that I cannot pursue here what is to Owen an "agonizingly uninteresting" idea, since however banal it may now seem it is of some importance from the point of view of cultural history. But, briefly, Guo Shaoyu in discussing Jiaoran and Hanshan adds little to what has already been said. Wang Meng'ou, in addition to a similar mention of Jiaoran, cites Wang Changling interestingly, but this poet touches on Buddhist philosophy of language, not Zen. He also cites more appositely Dai Shulun, over whose works there hover questions of authenticity, and the monk-poet Qiji, a figure of the late Tang. I am therefore inclined to see the "search for unity" between Zen and poetry as part of a larger reconciliation of Buddhist and Chinese culture, but one which becomes visible more in the generation following Jiaoran, for example in the writings of Liu Zongyuan (773–819).

64. See Robert E. Buswell, Jr, *The Korean Approach to Zen: The Collected Works of Chinul* (Honolulu: University of Hawaii Press, 1983), pp.16–17. Bernard Faure, *The Rhetoric of Immediacy* (Princeton: Princeton University Press, 1991), has done much to explain the particular verbal tics of the Zen tradition which have been a source of great confusion in the past.

65. T. Griffith Foulk, on pp.154 and 180 of his "Myth, Ritual and Monastic Practice in Sung Ch'an Buddhism", in *Religion and Society in T'ang and Sung China*, ed. Patricia Buckley Ebrey and Peter N. Gregory (Honolulu: University of Hawaii Press, 1993), pp.147–208, stresses the way in which the Chan tradition provided entirely Chinese Buddha equivalents for Chinese Buddhists of this period; the Indian background of Buddhism thus became in a sense an irrelevance.

66. Peter K. Bol, *This Culture of Ours: Intellectual Transitions in T'ang and Sung China* (Stanford: Stanford University Press, 1992), covers the shift from the point of view of the literati and their culture.

67. Despite a number of useful studies, the emergence of Buddhist literary culture has not been covered by any one monographic survey. Most pertinent of shorter pieces is Robert M. Gimello, "Mārga and Culture: Learning, Letters and Liberation in Northern Sung Ch'an", in Robert E. Buswell, Jr, and Robert M. Gimello, *Paths to Liberation: The Mārga and its Transformations in Buddhist Thought* (Honolulu: University of Hawaii Press, 1992), pp.371–437. This topic is also the subject of current research by George A. Keyworth of the University of California at Los Angeles.

68. Mark Robert Halperin, "Pieties and Responsibilities: Buddhism and the Chinese Literati, 780–1280" (Ph.D. dissertation, University of California at Berkeley, 1997).

69. According to Komazawa University, ed., *Zengaku daijiten* (Tokyo: Taishukan, 1978), p.686b; its quotation from the earlier master Mazu Daoyi cannot be established as deriving from any early source.

70. See his *Chanyuan zhuquanji duxu*, 2B, p.412c in the edition of the Taishō Canon, vol.48; he does not, of course, himself contrast "High" and "Broad" as I have done, but speaks in the latter case of "echoes of Zen", rather than Zen itself. On this text, see Gregory, *Tsung-mi*, pp.315-16.

71. The definitive collection of early Zen verse was to become that contained in fascicles 29 and 30 of Daoyuan, *Jingde chuandenglu*, pp.449-67, in the edition of the Taishō Canon, vol.51; the relationship of this collection with Zongmi's earlier editorial efforts in drawing up a "Zen Canon" is yet to be fully explored. On Daoyuan's compilation, see Isshū Miura and Ruth Fuller Sasaki, *Zen Dust* (New York: Harcourt, Brace and World, 1966), pp.350-52. For developments of the Hanshan legend in this text, see Wu, "Study", pp.419-20.

72. Wu, "Study", pp.395-7. Wu would place the latter figure in a text of the early eighth century, but since that text is lost, the safest date is that of the tenth-century source that cites it.

73. Li Yi, *Chanjia Hanshan shi zhu* (Taibei: Zhengzhong shuju, 1992), pp.661-2, cites (following earlier sources) positive remarks on Hanshan attributed (apparently correctly; cf. p.669) to the great Confucian Zhu Xi (1130-1200) and the poet Lu You (1125-1210). These commendations were never included in the formal Collected Works of either man. The *shihua* literature does not entirely ignore Hanshan, as will be seen below, but the exceptions are interestingly limited.

74. Note the allusion in Chuyuan, comp., *Fenyang Wude chanshi yulu*, A, p.597c in the edition of the Taishō Canon, vol.47; this text contains the sayings of Wude (947-1024); cf. Miura and Sasaki, *Zen Dust*, pp.355-6. I owe the reference to unpublished work (forthcoming in *T'oung pao*) by George Keyworth. For an early quotation of Hanshan by name, citing one of the poems using what Pulleyblank terms a late rhyme scheme, see Yanshou (904-75), *Zhu Xinfu*, 1, p.23 recto-b, in the edition of *Xu zangjing*, 2A 16/1, and see Henricks, *Poetry of Hanshan*, p.231, no.160.

75. See James Cahill, *An Index of Early Chinese Painters and Paintings* (Berkeley: University of California Press, 1980), pp.39, 46 (Fenggan), 97, 130, 140, 171, 226-7, 357, 359, 360, 361 and 368. Tracing the success of Hanshan's visual image would take us rather far afield: paired with Shide, he became so well known as to be treated as a minor god of riches in popular religion; see Wolfram Eberhard, *A Dictionary of Chinese Symbols* (London: Routledge & Kegan Paul, 1986), pp.142 (s.v. "He-he"), 251-2.

76. For the printing of this work, see below, n.80.

77. Cf. F.W. Mote, "Confucian Eremitism in the Yüan Period", in *The Confucian Persuasion*, ed. A.F. Wright (Stanford: Stanford University Press, 1960), pp.202-40.

78. This was of course by no means universally the case: for two exceptions see the essays by Jan Yün-hua and Chün-fang Yü in *Yüan Thought: Chinese Thought and Religion under the Mongols*, ed. Hok-lam Chan and W. Theodore de Bary (New York: Columbia University Press, 1982), pp.375-477.

79. See Ling Chung, "The Reception of Cold Mountain's Poetry in the Far East and the United States", in *China and the West: Comparative Literature Studies*, ed. William Tay, Ying-hsiung Chou and Heh-hsiang Yuan (Hong Kong: The Chinese University Press, 1980), pp.85-96 (on pp.86-7): "These poems were not included in the government-sponsored collections of Buddhist writings."

80. Cf. the (Taiwan) *Zhonghua dazangjing*, 2nd series, text 103 – not in the microfilm catalogue of the Jingshan Canon issued by the National Central Library, Taibei, as List no.20, 1981, nor in *Ershiwu zhong zangjing mulu duichao kaoshi* (Taibei: Xinwenfeng, 1983), the synthetic catalogue of the various editions of the Canon by the veteran

Buddhist bibliographer Cai Yunchen. It must be said, however, that the Jingshan Canon was issued over such a long time-span and in such a haphazard way that its contents are difficult to define.

81. *Zhonghua dazangjing*, 2nd series, text 283. Text 293 is a further collection of imitations, but in this case without the originals. For some lesser sets of imitations, including those of Wang Anshi (1021–86), see Li, *Chanjia Hanshan shi zhu*, pp.703–15.

82. Yongzheng's anthology has been reprinted several times in canonical collections and independently; Hanshan occupies fascicle 4, *Yuxuan yulu*, of this 40-volume work. A recent typeset edition has been included in the series *Foguang dazangjing: Chanzang* (Gaoxiong, Taiwan, 1994).

83. The imperial preface (p.83 in the edition cited in the preceding note) considers the case for regarding the poems as "popular" verse, as mere rhymes, as doctrinal verse, or as Zen verse, and rejects all these possibilities. Instead, the Yongzheng emperor claims for himself the role of true interpreter of their spirit by citing Hanshan's prediction that one day he would be understood (cf. Henricks, p.410, and p.405, n.3).

84. Five poems are addressed to Hanshan in fascicle 6 of his Collected Sayings alone, *Xutang heshang yulu*, pp.1030–33, in the edition of the Taishō Canon, vol.47. For the history of his writings, cf. Miura and Sasaki, *Zen Dust*, pp.361–2.

85. Ivo Smits, *The Pursuit of Loneliness: Chinese and Japanese Nature Poetry in Medieval Japan, ca.1050–1150* (Wiesbaden: Steiner, 1995), pp.41–2. The Japanese visitor to China whom Smits points to as a possible transmitter of Hanshan's verse also preserves an interesting early version of his legend: cf. Robert Borgen, "The Legend of Hanshan: A Neglected Source", *Journal of the American Oriental Society* 111 (1991), pp.575–9.

86. See Yoshida Toyoko, "Chinese Aloneness and Japanese Loneliness: The Poetry of Han Shan and Saigyō", *Transactions of the Asiatic Society of Japan* (1981), pp.57–75 (on pp.57–8).

87. On these centres, see Martin Collcutt, *Five Mountains: The Rinzai Zen Monastic Institution in Medieval Japan* (Cambridge, MA: Harvard University Press, 1981), although this study concerns institutions more than culture.

88. See Alain-Louis Colas, *Poèmes du Zen des Cinq-Montagnes* (Paris: Maisonneuve et Larose, 1991), p.4. Collcutt (preceding note), p.63, speaks of only a "brief hiatus" in cultural exchange caused by the Mongol invasion.

89. See Henricks, p.227. For the cat as companion to monks, cf. T.H. Barrett, *The Religious Affiliations of the Chinese Cat: An Essay Towards an Anthropozoological Approach to Comparative Religion* (London: School of Oriental and African Studies, University of London, 1998; Louis Jordan Occasional Paper, 2), pp.12–16.

90. Marian Ury, *Poems of the Five Mountains: An Introduction to the Literature of the Zen Monasteries* (Ann Arbor: Center for Japanese Studies, University of Michigan, 1992), p.73, translating a fifteenth-century poet. Xutang Zhiyu, it should be noted, would have already introduced cat poems to Japan – but in writing in this vein he may have been following Hanshan anyhow. I hope to produce a study of this minor intellectual current in due course.

91. Ueda Makoto, *Bashō and his Interpreters: Selected Hokku with Commentary* (Stanford: Stanford University Press, 1992), pp.85, 346–7.

92. Since the postwar shift initiated by Iriya Yoshitaka towards an interest in the problem of Hanshan's colloquial grammar, the reputation of the traditional commentaries, which pay no attention to this issue, have suffered as a consequence. Yamaguchi Harumichi, "*Kanzanshi kō*", *Indogaku Bukkyōgaku kenkyū* 18.2 (1970), pp.784–6, introduces briefly but more sympathetically the main achievements of Tokugawa scholarship on Hanshan.

93. See John Stevens, trans., *Dewdrops on a Lotus Leaf: Zen Poems of Ryokan* (Boston and London: Shambhala, 1993), p.19.

94. Komazawa University, comp., *Zengaku daijiten* (Tokyo: Taishukan, 1978), p.180a.
95. Chiang Yee, *The Silent Traveller in Edinburgh* (London: Methuen, 1948), pp.89–90; apparently unaware of the Japanese origins of the bell, he takes this as a straightforward case of looting.
96. Wu, "Study", pp.421–2.
97. Yu Yue, *Chunzaitang suibi* 6 (Huaiyang: Jiangsu renmin chubanshe, 1984), p.92.
98. Thanks to the generosity of Dr Anne Cheng, I possess a small penknife bearing the images of Hanshan and Shide on one side and Zhang Ji's poem on the other – a souvenir both useful and instructive.
99. The editions of Hanshan form a highly technical topic unsuitable for detailed treatment here: Wu, "Study", p.446, gives a greatly condensed chart showing the place of the fourteenth-century Korean edition according to his understanding of the textual history of the corpus.
100. Nguyen Cuong Tu, *Zen in Medieval Vietnam* (Honolulu: University of Hawaii Press, 1997), pp.126–7.
101. See above, nn.80 and 81 (in all cases these allegations are made, as politeness would seem to have demanded, in the prefaces), and cf. the materials assembled in Wu, "Study".
102. See p.134 of Reginald Johnston, "Han-shan (Kanzan) and Shih-te (Jittoku) in Chinese and Japanese Literature and Art", *Transactions and Proceedings of the Japan Society* 34 (1936–7), pp.133–7. Something of the Hanshan spirit seems to have kept Sir Reginald somewhat aloof from SOAS, and eventually no closer than Scotland: see Robert Bickers, "Coolie Work: Sir Reginald Johnston at the School of Oriental Studies, 1931–1937", *Journal of the Royal Asiatic Society*, 3rd series, 5 (1995), pp.385–401.
103. Ling Chung, "Reception of Cold Mountain", pp.90–91.
104. He, *Lidai shihua*, pp.393, 793; see also n.27 above for the "Madman of Chu" comparison.
105. Demiéville, *Wang*, p.607, puts the last known citations from his poems in the late twelfth century. Note among the citations, pp.595–6, an instance of confusion between Wang and Hanshan; at one point they were evidently quite closely associated in some people's minds.
106. Miura and Sasaki, *Zen Dust*, pp.390–91, covers the history of these materials, but does not bring out the terminology used by the editor of 1143, which implies a fair degree of intervention. Obviously it is easier to upgrade prose than verse, which is tied to rhyme structures.
107. One recent study that attempts to grapple with this signal difference between Chinese and European literatures is Eva Shan Chou, *Reconsidering Tu Fu: Literary Greatness and Cultural Context* (Cambridge: Cambridge University Press, 1995), but the problem is not confined to this poet alone.
108. Nishitani's work is explained in the accompanying survey on "Hanshan in translation".
109. Nguyen, *Zen in Medieval Vietnam*, pp.63, 66.

Hanshan in translation

Anyone who has been intrigued by the poems published in this volume will probably welcome guidance on where to find a translation of the entire corpus of the poetry. Two such translations are available in English, but the reader should be warned that whoever first adopted the name Hanshan was to all appearances a somewhat uneven poet, and that there is reliable evidence that a fair proportion of the poems in the total corpus of slightly over 300 pieces are actually by a later hand, or hands. Although any anthology reflects no more than the sensibilities of its compiler, the number of further gems to be discovered in these complete translations is proportionally smaller than appears here, and some items under Hanshan's name (quite possibly including correct attributions) can only be termed verse rather than poetry.

That said, several reviewers have commended both the accuracy and spirit of the following translation, the work of a pseudonymous hermit in the true Hanshan tradition, which I have not been able to consult:

Red Pine, *The Collected Songs of Cold Mountain* (Port Townsend, WA: Copper Canyon Press, 1983).

But there are also reasons to cite another complete translation that has been seen as less inspired. The following volume is amply equipped with annotations to the poems, as well as some useful appendices (including a concordance to four other partial translations) and a good bibliography of both Western and East Asian literature:

Robert G. Henricks, *The Poetry of Han-shan: A Complete, Annotated Translation of Cold Mountain* (Albany, NY: State University of New York Press, 1990).

The numbering of the poems in Henricks's translation follows their ordering in the entire corpus of Tang-dynasty poetry, as collected in the eighteenth century by imperial command:

147

Peng Dingqiu, ed., *Quan Tang shi* (Beijing: Zhonghua shuju, 1960, and reprints); Hanshan occupies fascicle 806, pp.9063–102, in this edition.

One advantage of Henricks's work is that it relies on the most careful complete translation into a foreign language available: the following Japanese study identifies not only the obvious allusions that puzzle every foreign reader but also those more hidden allusions and references which can be detected only by someone immersed in the literature of medieval China:

Iritani Sensuke and Matsumura Takeshi, *Kanzanshi*, Zen no goroku, vol.13 (Tokyo: Chikuma shobō, 1970).

To facilitate the use of Henricks's translation as a study guide, his enumeration is shown in parentheses at the head of all Peter Hobson's translations printed in the present volume. It should, however, be pointed out that Henricks's translations have been criticized at length for not capturing the nuances of Hanshan's frequently colloquial (not to say slangy) diction, in the following review article:

Victor Mair, "Script and Word in Medieval Vernacular Sinitic", *Journal of the American Oriental Society* 112.2 (1992), pp.269–78.

Another substantial review, which draws attention to the role of poetic convention throughout the corpus and argues the case against any attempt to identify a single individual even as the original Hanshan – other than to point out links with the school of Buddhism (not Zen) predominant in the locality – is:

Stephen R. Bokenkamp, in *Chinese Literature: Essays, Articles and Reviews* 3.3 (1991), pp.619–24.

For a greater number of translations into English than are accounted for in Henricks's appendix the reader is referred to the following list, which uses the *Quan Tang shi* enumeration as found also in the Henricks versions (in parentheses, as has been done here):

Sydney S.K. Fung and S.T. Lai, comp., *25 T'ang Poets: Index to English Translations* (Shatin, NT, Hong Kong: The Chinese University Press, 1984); Hanshan occupies pp.19–31.

A fuller bibliography of Western-language studies and translations than that given by Henricks may be found on pp.61–3 of:

William H. Nienhauser, Jr, ed., *Bibliography of Selected Western Works on T'ang Dynasty Literature* (Taibei: Center for Chinese Studies, 1988).

All the sources of information cited above are of course already a little dated, given the penchant of most anthologists for including some samples of Hanshan. One recent example of Hanshan finding his place in the over-all history of Chinese literature may be found on pp.404–6 of:

Stephen Owen, *An Anthology of Chinese Literature: Beginnings to 1911* (New York: Norton, 1996).

Beyond English-language publications, the number of omissions from bibliographies of material concerning Hanshan may be even greater. The following selection of translations with Chinese text, for example, is listed by neither Henricks nor Nienhauser:

Hervé Collet and Cheng Wing fan, *Han Shan: 108 poèmes* (Millemont: Moundarren, 1985).

As for scholarship in East Asian languages, the best that can be said is that a steady stream of publications on this corpus of poetry continues to appear year by year. Among monographic studies of the type listed by Henricks, one representative more recent edition, attractively printed with useful appendices but disappointingly annotated, is:

Li Yi, ed., *Chanjia Hanshan shi zhu* (Taibei: Zhengzhong shuju, 1992).

Of Japanese studies, attention should be drawn particularly to the follow-ing omission, since despite acknowledging that the Hanshan corpus cannot be treated as Zen poetry as such, the commentator has chosen a small selec-tion of poems (about a third of the number in the present volume) and argued at least for the validity of a Zen approach to their interpretation:

Nishitani Keiji, "Kanzan shi", in *Zenke goroku*, ed. Nishitani Keiji and Yanagida Seizan (Tokyo: Chikuma shobō, 1974), pp.5–112.

In addition, readers may wish to know something of the literary context of Peter Hobson's work. Three of the poems included here (nos.101–3) were printed, as "Three Short Poems by Han-shan", in *Studies in Com-parative Religion* 11.2 (spring 1977), pp.83–4, as far as we have been able to tell under his own copyright. This periodical was published from Pates Manor, Bedfont, Middlesex, by F. Clive-Ross, and, after his death, by Olive Clive-Ross and Hobson himself. The final issue, volume 17.1/2, seems to have appeared in 1987; a review by Hobson on p.127 gives his views on translation as already reported in the Introduction (p.2). Other contributions by him may be found throughout its pages, from "Some Observations on Indonesian Textiles", *Studies in Comparative Religion*

7.3 (summer 1973), pp.162–73, to "The Three-Character Rhymed Classic on the Ka'bah", *Studies in Comparative Religion* 14.3/4 (spring–autumn 1980), pp.181–94.

One of Hobson's translations, "'The Far Journey': An Archaic Chinese Poem", *Studies in Comparative Religion* 15.1/2 (spring 1983), pp.42–53, specifically acknowledges a debt to the research of a Japanese scholar, Hoshikawa Kiyotaka. I am confident that in preparing his translations of Hanshan he also made extensive use of the following work:

Iriya Yoshitaka, *Kanzan shi*, Chūgoku shijin senshū, vol.5 (Tokyo: Iwanami, 1958).

The reason for this assertion is not simply the high degree of overlap between Hobson's translations and the selection commented on by Iriya. Nor is it the fact that a quick survey of his library arranged for me in July 1999, through the courtesy of his nephew, Dr Tim Jones, and Jones's parents, revealed no other book on Hanshan. On pp.157–8 of Iriya's Japanese anthology a poem is presented which is, uniquely, not by Hanshan but by his supposed Zen companion, Shide: this poem duly appears as no.67 in Hobson's own anthology. Given that Iriya was a pioneer in rendering the colloquial nuances in this type of poetry which, as noted above, have been overlooked by some other translators (and all traditional commentators), we can be sure that, whatever the final outcome of Hobson's efforts at translation, he did use the best available guide to the actual meaning of the poems. Another anthology that is linked to Iriya's work is the following:

Burton Watson, *Cold Mountain: 100 Poems by the T'ang Poet Han-shan* (New York: Columbia University Press, 1970).

Watson worked closely with Iriya; it is perhaps fair to say that the results, while quite reliable, are less individualistic than those published here. A review of the first edition of Watson's work (New York: Grove Press, 1962) by David Hawkes may be found in the *Journal of the American Oriental Society* 82.4 (December 1962), pp.596–9; it includes pioneering finding lists similar to those published by Henricks, but in this case keyed to the editions of Hanshan published in the Sibu congkan, a major Chinese reprint series.

Besides the lengthy reviews already mentioned, one or two independent studies comparing translations from Hanshan already exist, though the most comprehensive known to me was published before the appearance of the Henricks volume. This is Paul Kahn, "Han Shan in English", *Renditions* 25 (spring 1986), pp.140–75. This was reprinted in a slightly extended version as a slim volume under the same title (Buffalo, New York: White Pine Press, 1989). Perhaps the appearance of Peter Hobson's utterly individual recreations of the Chinese will prompt some further thoughts on the topic, from Mr Kahn or from others.

It seems likely that in Hanshan scholarship and appreciation "one hundred flowers" will continue to blossom: there can be no sense in which the translations offered here may be taken as definitive. Even so, they certainly bloom as colourfully and fragrantly as any. Peter Hobson was, after all, a man who knew from first hand about public service, and also about retreat from it. He did not select a mountain hermitage for his retirement, but he did use his time to explore religious questions. Had he and Hanshan ever met, I am sure they would have enjoyed each other's company and found much to talk about. Every volume of translation, whether overtly or not, introduces the reader to two literary personalities. I hope that in this case both of them will be found at the same time distinctive and engaging.